APPROACHING RETIREMENT

a Consumer Publication

Consumers' Association
publishers of **Which?**
2 Marylebone Road
London NW1 4DX

CONTENTS

FOREWORD

Retiring from work is likely to bring with it the most sudden and fundamental change in lifestyle you have ever experienced. But like all important events in life, planning ahead will make the transition a much more ordered affair. Some people are so immersed in their work and work environment that they can only see retirement as a desired release from routine. They may not appreciate that new routines will have to be learned and new disciplines acquired, without which they risk squandering that most valuable commodity, time.

Before retiring, your time is rarely your own, and thus the free time brought by a weekend or a holiday is treasured as it deserves. Retirement is potentially a full-time holiday, which may last for ten, twenty years or even much longer. Some people live almost as long in retirement as they were previously in employment. And just as vocational training enhances your abilities in employment, proper preparation for retirement will help to maximise the enjoyment which it brings.

Retirement will bring the need to adjust in other ways. Financially, you are unlikely to be able to enjoy the same standard of living as hitherto, and inflation may make inroads on the real value of your savings; the years may also take their toll of your health. But if you can anticipate such problems, you can lessen their impact on your enjoyment of life.

An ageing population, coupled with increased life expectancy and greater affluence, will give rise to a substantial retirement industry in the next decade or so. Signs of this are already apparent. The holiday industry is catering for the retired population by providing very cheap out-of-season accommodation on the Mediterranean – an arrangement that is no doubt of mutual benefit financially. There are now specialist providers of accommodation for those who no longer wish to shoulder all of the burdens of managing their own homes.

Perhaps one day there will be professional retirement counsellors, just as today there are job counsellors. But for the moment the pensioner still remains a largely neglected member of society.

You will need to be prepared for important changes in the quality and pace of life. Here we try to help you to look ahead and meet the challenge.

THINKING ABOUT THE MONEY

It is essential to think about your future finances well before you retire – five years or more ahead, if you can; even two years ahead is better than nothing.

Try to make as detailed a forecast as possible of what your likely income will be when you stop work and how much money you will need to spend on what. Also consider how your spending pattern is likely to change.

It is difficult to make financial predictions long before your retirement, and particularly difficult to take account of inflation. However, you can – and should – revise your estimate regularly.

income

You will almost certainly have less income when you retire. Instead of a regular salary or wages and perhaps income from savings you will have to rely on

○ a basic state retirement pension (for a single person or a married couple)
○ maybe an addition to your state pension, related to what you earned while employed
○ possibly an occupational pension from your employer, or for a self-employed person a personal pension
○ the income from any savings and investments (because of inflation and fluctuations, it is generally sensible to make a pessimistic estimate)
○ other sources, such as any earnings from freelance part-time jobs.

inflation
The value of money is likely to continue going down. Although certain investments and some pensions are inflation-linked, salaries and wages are more likely to keep pace with inflation than do pensions, so the effect will be more noticeable. If inflation is 5%, for a sum to be worth £1,000 at today's prices, it would need to be £1,628 at the end of 10 years, and £2,079 at the end of 15 years. Even if inflation is only 3%, the 10-year and 15-year figures would be £1,344 and £1,558 respectively.

spending

If you have never done any domestic budgeting, now is the time to start jotting down what your current spending pattern is. Keep a careful detailed record for a few months – ideally for a whole year – of what you really spend (preferably day by day, or week by week). This will show you exactly where your money goes now, and highlight how much you really need to spend on

○ everyday items you buy regularly (food and drink, household goods, newspapers, clothes, petrol, cigarettes)
○ regular lump sums, for bills which come in regularly and at predictable intervals (the rates, mortgage, road tax, fuel bills, TV licence, telephone)
○ leisure activities (books, cinema, pub, gardening, sports and hobbies)
○ presents (birthdays, Christmas, family happenings)
○ irregular lump sums (for major items such as holidays, new washing machine, redecorating the house)
○ unforseeable expenditure (major car repairs, a leaking roof, other major repairs).

If you know how you spend your money, you may be able to see where you could economise, if necessary, and what could be cut out altogether.

Bear in mind the likely change in your spending pattern when you retire. Some of this relates to simply stopping work. For example, you will not have to pay fares to and from work, or buy lunch out. Alternatively, you may find that you need to spend more on food if you usually have lunch at a subsidised canteen.

When drawing up your budget, also take into account the effect of simply growing older. In your late sixties, you may want (or will need) to spend more than you do now on heating, on labour-saving appliances, on transport, including taxis. Look several years ahead and allow for age-related changes in spending, so as to be realistic when you work out your future budget. Do not assume you will spend your money in the same way as you did in your forties or fifties.

what will be different

Changes in your spending are likely because

○ by the time you retire your children will probably have left home and be financially independent
○ you will probably be free of your mortgage
○ payments into a personal pension scheme are likely to have ended
○ you may want to plan your holidays differently – travel in more comfort perhaps, or spend more on trips abroad – on the other hand, you may be able to save by being able to travel during the off-season and at reduced fares
○ when you are at home all day in the winter, your heating bill will go up and it is likely that the telephone bill will too; many people use the phone at work, and sometimes stationery and other office facilities

○ you may be spending less on food when you do not have to rely on quickly prepared but expensive convenience food or frozen meals, but you may end up spending more money on special ingredients and on gas or electricity

○ there will be more time for 'entertaining' – inviting friends for drinks or a meal is enjoyable but also costs money; when invitations are reciprocated, that may not save any money, however enjoyable it is

○ there will be more time for leisure activities which cost money (theatres, concerts, films) but you may be able to take advantage of price concessions (for example, cheaper tickets for 'first house' cinema or theatre matinees)

○ more time for gardening may mean growing your own vegetables more successfully; the seeds cost very little, and you can save the cost of fertilizers by making your own compost, of insecticides by spraying with soap solution, of weedkillers by removing weeds by hand

○ the need for clothes will change: being retired does not mean that you have to go around looking dowdy, but there will be less need for formal clothing, you may find that you spend less on smart clothes than when you were working. However, as people get older, they often need to spend more on warm clothing

○ you may no longer be prepared to walk in the pouring rain and will pay out more for bus rides and even the occasional taxi (but there may well be fare concessions to take advantage of).

A major cost, which cannot be postponed indefinitely after retirement, is having to replace appliances and household equipment as it, too, gets old. While you are still earning it is worth assessing if anything will need to be replaced before too long – refrigerator, washing machine, bed, cooker. This may also be a good time to think about the car.

a gap between income and spending

If it seems that you will need more money than you are going to have in retirement, the solutions include

○ spending less now on inessentials, so that you can save up for retirement while you still have a regular income
○ making additional voluntary contributions (AVCs) towards your pension
○ finding ways of increasing your income after retirement, by reorganising your investments to give income later
○ planning to take part-time work after retirement, if you can find it
○ moving to a smaller or less expensive home.

WHERE TO LIVE

While you are working, where you live is necessarily affected to a significant extent by where your place of work is. At 50-plus, the fact of your approaching retirement should act as a spur for you to consider whether you will still wish to live there when you are at liberty (subject only to financial constraints) to move elsewhere. You should take plenty of time to decide. If you have it in mind to move to a particular area of the country, perhaps an area that you know from holidaying there, make a point of getting to know it better. Never move just for the sake of moving house, only do so because you know that the advantages to be gained by moving outweigh any disadvantages of staying.

do you need to move . . . ?

If you think that you are going to want to move, start by asking yourself, and answering honestly, questions about your present home. This should help you decide whether it is the house itself or the neighbourhood that you want to leave. And if you already have another home in mind, ask yourself the same questions about it.

- Is your home large enough, light enough, warm enough, comfortable enough?
- Do you like your house or flat and the area in which you live? Your experience of your home may be very different when you are not at work on weekdays. If your neighbours have children, remember that children are by definition

both noisy and boisterous, and like to play outside; they also have holidays long enough to drive their parents to distraction. Might they drive you to distraction too?

○ Is there someone in the neighbourhood who carries on a noisy or offensive business in his back yard? Is your neighbour an amateur or even a professional musician who practices all day long? If your house is terraced or semi-detached, or only a few feet from the house next door, just how effectively do its walls insulate you from sound? While you can reasonably expect noise to be kept to a moderate level at night time, few people exercise any such restraints during the day.

○ Do members of your family live nearby?

○ Would you mind having to leave your friends in the neighbourhood? It may not be easy to make new friends if you move away.

○ Just how close at hand are the local shops, post office, library, club, church and other facilities – distance matters less while you are fit and able to drive a car.

○ How busy is the traffic in the area (from the pedestrian or the driver's point of view).

garden

Look particularly at the garden – is it large enough for your future gardening plans? Will it be too large to manage on your own in five, ten, twenty years time?

Traditionally, gardening is high on the list of a retired person's activities, but if you dislike it or have always found it a chore, a large garden might be one factor in deciding to move. Not at the time of retirement but later on, when you are older, a garden can become a great anxiety. Even a beloved garden may become a burden when everything grows faster than it can be controlled.

You could perhaps rid yourself of unwanted space by obtaining planning permission to build on it, and then sell it off with planning permission, or you might even build a new house or bungalow for yourself in the garden/grounds of your house, and then sell off the house.

Gardening involves quite hard physical work; bending and lifting get more difficult as people get older, particularly for someone suffering from arthritis. Perhaps your garden can be converted into an easy-care garden with minimal flower beds, no vegetable plots, more perennials.

A garden can be adapted to make it easier for a disabled or elderly person to manage, perhaps by changing the layout or building raised flower beds. There are tools that reduce the amount of stooping, reaching and bending, and special lightweight tools. Ways of making the work easier are sitting down to some jobs that are usually done standing, changing jobs frequently so that it is not necessary to stay in one position for a long time, stopping before getting tired.

For advice on planning the garden, tools and techniques for older people write to **Horticultural Therapy**, Goulds Ground, Vallis Way, Frome, Somerset BA11 3DW.

At the **Gardening Centre**, Syon Park, Brentford, Middlesex, there is a demonstration garden for the disabled and elderly (run by Horticultural Therapy). This includes raised beds and other suggested ways of planting; a greenhouse which allows entry for a wheelchair and has propagating shelves within easy reach, and a selection of suitable garden tools. Demonstrations can be arranged on wednesdays and fridays, by appointment. There is also a garden designed for the disabled at Battersea Park in London and a disabled and sight and sound garden at **Capel Manor Horticultural and Environmental Centre**, Bullsmore Lane, Waltham Cross, Herts EN7 5HR.

Gardening in Retirement by Isobel Pays is published by Age Concern (£1.95). A report *Planning for less work* was published in the September 1988 issue of *Gardening from Which?*.

If you sell your house, and do not want to leave behind some mature plants, you should have the purchaser's agreement to your removing any plants you want to take with you.

the size of the house

One reason for considering a move may be that the present home is, or is likely to become, too big.

If your children have left and you are still working, you may think your three or four bedroomed house too big for just two of you, but a house of this size may be very convenient for two people who are at home all day. Space-taking activities are likely to expand with more leisure, and couples often find that a room of their own each, where they can perhaps just write letters undisturbed, or leave the hobby ready to take up again later, is an excellent use of extra rooms.

It is worth looking at your present home afresh, to see if the rooms could be more usefully arranged. The present arrangement of one bedroom, one dining room, one sitting room and one spare room could become two bedsitters, one study and a lounge with a large dining area.

Turning a spare bedroom into a workshop for d-i-y activities may be useful; the room will have electric sockets, possibly a water supply and will be a place to work in comfort without disrupting the rest of the household – and without having to clear up. Similarly, a small room where the sewing machine, and all that goes with it, can be left out permanently ready to use, and where a tailor's dummy will not be in anyone's way, may be a useful transformation from what used to be one of the children's bedrooms. If you transform all the spare rooms, however, try to make sure that you will still have room for visitors. And if you have visiting family who drop in for an overnight stay from time to time, you will need an extra room, anyway.

For a house that is big and likely to become too expensive to run or maintain on your reduced income, you might – with great caution – consider sharing it with friends or members of the family. If you are thinking of taking lodgers, beware of the problems of getting rid of troublesome tenants. The Consumer Publication *Renting and letting* gives advice on this. It may be possible, with some investment, to convert a house into two flats and sell or let one.

You may think that your present house will eventually become too difficult to manage. It may have inconvenient stairs to climb, a lot of windows and floors to keep clean, a heating system that is not adequate or economical when you are at home all day.

Apart from the expense of a house and garden, and the worry about not having enough money for the necessary maintenance and repairs, when you get older you may feel exhausted and depressed by the physical struggle to keep a large old house cleaned, heated, and in good repair.

On the other hand, maybe your accommodation now seems too small: a flat may have been quite adequate while you were at work, but when you are retired and spend much more time at home, a couple of rooms may not be enough.

But if you are thinking about moving to a larger place, consider carefully whether you have enough furniture, and enough money and energy to start a new type of home.

improving and adapting the home

If you decide not to move, think about comfort and safety in the home and necessary repairs and possible improvements before you retire, while you have an income to cover any major expense. Now is the time for undertaking major decorations and maintenance and installing new equipment.

Do not delay too long before dealing with house maintenance. The longer you wait before repairing a broken gutter or a leaking roof, the more consequential damage will occur and the more expensive the repair will be. It may be worth having a professional structural survey carried out on the house to identify major and substantial repairs. A report on outdoor maintenance is published in *Which?* April 1989.

bathroom
In a large house it may be possible, and would probably be very useful for later years, to install an extra downstairs lavatory (if there is not one already on the ground floor) and a basin or even a shower.

The existing bathroom may also need attention. Consider having a shower installed which uses less hot water than a bath and is therefore more economical. If a new bath is needed, choose one suitable for an older person – lower than usual baths, for example, are available and also baths with a lower section in the middle of one side.

If you are thinking of fitting a bath rail, a horizontal one at hip height is a good general purpose rail. A handrail beside the lavatory may become necessary if an older person loses muscle power. A diagonal rail is a useful multi-purpose one: it conforms to the pattern of movement of standing and sitting. Make sure that any rail is very securely fixed by someone skilled at the job who knows the structure of the walls. Any grab rail, wherever it is fitted, must be firmly enough attached to be able to take the strain of the body's weight.

The **Disabled Living Foundation**, 380/384 Harrow Road, London W9 2HU (telephone 01-289 6111) can be asked for advice and a list of suppliers.

electricity
If you have not had the wiring checked in the last ten years, have that done now by a competent electrician and, if necessary, have the house or flat rewired, and perhaps extra circuits

put in. The local electricity board or an independent qualified electrician can be asked to carry out a safety inspection on the wiring, which may be free of charge if you want a quotation for rewiring the house.

If you are having any electrical work done, it might be a good idea to have new sockets put in at convenient places and heights, where they are easy to reach, perhaps waist-high so that you do not have to stoop. A socket protected by an RCD (residual current device) is a very useful safety measure, particularly if electricity is used in the garden or a workshop (portable RCD plugs or adaptors are also available).

safety and convenience
Make sure that there is adequate lighting in every area of the house and especially on the stairs. With two-way switches, you do not need to enter the house or cross the hallway or use the stairs in the dark.

Most kitchens could be made more convenient, and safer. A new cooker is an expensive piece of equipment, so if yours has become inefficient, it may be worth replacing it now with a new, split-level one with a separate oven, which saves having to bend down to lift out hot dishes.

Shelves and cupboards are often too high or too low, so give some thought to reorganising what you keep where, to avoid having to bend, stretch or use steps too often. A strong pair of steps, preferably with a platform and handrail is useful – get in the habit of using them instead of doing a stretch-and-balance act on the kitchen stool.

A smoke alarm is not expensive and can be very easily fitted in any house. Remember to review the security arrangements of your home. It may be worth contacting your local police station, by telephone or by going there in person, to make an appointment for the local crime prevention officer to come to your home and carry out a security survey inside and outside the house. He should be able to give you detailed advice on how to make your home more secure. The police do not charge for advice from the crime prevention officer.

staying on in old age

The charity Help the Aged has a 'gifted house' scheme: you give the house to Help the Aged but continue to live there, rent free and with no responsibility for maintenance and repairs (internal or external), upkeep of garden, building insurance or payment of rates. Help the Aged will care for you for life and if later on you wish to, you can move to accommodation within the Help the Aged's other housing developments.

A booklet giving details, *Gifted housing plan*, is available from **Help the Aged**, 13 High Street, Horley, Surrey RH6 7BH.

moving in retirement?

SOME PROS

can choose your 'dream' home

smaller house
– cheaper to manage

bigger house
– more room for hobbies
– friends and relatives to stay

move closer to family

buy cheaper property to have a lump sum left over

other areas may offer more concessions

have a garden at long last

get rid of the garden at last

find a quieter, healthier environment

be able to have a pet

be able to have a garage or extra storage space

no service charges if from flat to house

SOME CONS

unfamiliar place, uncertainty
– may not be as idyllic as you imagined
  re public transport
  re possible isolation in winter
  overcrowding in summer

have to redecorate, may need new furniture

cost of move

distance from family and friends

maybe lose concessions

more responsibility for maintenance if from flat to house

may not be able to afford to move back if it doesn't work

Make your own list of pros and cons because it depends on where you are living now and where and what kind of place you are thinking of moving to, and why. If one column outweighs the other, it may give you a clearer idea of what you should consider doing.

what to do with your mortgage

Around two thirds of the houses or flats in Britain are owned by the people who live in them. But the chances are high that you, like most people, will have borrowed money in the form of a mortgage to help you to buy your own home.

Traditionally, mortgages are granted on the basis that they are paid off by the time the borrower reaches retirement age – either because an endowment mortgage 'matures' and pays out a lump sum to repay the loan, or, with a repayment mortgage, because the last instalment of the loan is repaid. But with the trend towards early retirement and with a rather more flexible attitude by lenders, this pattern is breaking down. The improvement in provision of pension schemes by employers means that many retired people now enjoy an income high enough to make it possible for them to continue to pay off a loan after retirement.

So there are several things to think about when you are approaching retirement:

o should you pay off your mortgage when you retire – possibly with a lump sum payment from your pension?
o should you pay off part of your mortgage?
o if you are considering moving, should you take out a new mortgage?

should you pay off your mortgage?

The answer to this question depends on your circumstances – whether you have a repayment or an endowment mortgage, what income you have, your tax rate, interest rates and so on.

But the first, and rather general point, is whether it is a 'good idea' to pay off a mortgage early. To pay off a mortgage, you must have a lump sum – this could be from an insurance policy, your pension, savings, a legacy and so on. The general principle is that it is worth using the lump sum to pay off the mortgage only if the rate of interest you are paying on the loan is higher than you can earn by investing that lump sum.

When working this out, remember that you are getting tax relief (at the highest rate of tax you pay) on the interest you pay on the first £30,000 of money you borrowed to buy your home. This reduces the rate of interest you are paying on the loan. For example, if the quoted mortgage rate is 12% and your highest rate of tax is the basic rate of 25%, the actual cost to you of the mortgage is only 9%; if you are paying tax at 40% it costs only 7.2%.

AFTER TAX-RELIEF INTEREST RATES

quoted rate	tax 25%	tax 40%
	after tax-relief rate	
10%	7.5%	6%
11%	8.25%	6.6%
12%	9%	7.2%
13%	9.75%	7.8%
14%	10.5%	8.4%

At the time of writing this book, the standard mortgage rate was 12.75% (equivalent to 9.6% for a basic rate tax payer) and it was possible to get 9.8% after basic rate tax even from a building society account. So at this time it was better to invest the money and use the interest to pay for the mortgage loan. Of course, the situation can change and it is worth keeping an eye on interest rates periodically to check that your decision is still correct.

If your mortgage is higher than £30,000 it may well be worth your reducing it to £30,000 if you can. This is because there is no tax relief on the amount of the loan over £30,000 and it may be hard to find an investment paying an after-tax return high enough to be able to pay the interest on that part of the loan.

One problem with this rather simple equation is that it ignores the fact that the actual interest rate, particularly on a repayment mortgage, is slightly higher than the quoted rate. The difference is fairly large over the last few years of a repayment mortgage (see page 27).

But if you do want to pay off even part of your loan, take into account the costs of doing this. For example, will you suffer a penalty for withdrawing other investments or pay charges, perhaps for selling shares? If you are to use part of a pension lump sum, are you losing more in pension than you would be paying out in repayments? All these are factors to consider.

if you have an endowment mortgage

With an endowment mortgage, you pay interest on the whole amount you borrowed to buy your home, over the whole length of your mortgage term. In addition, you pay premiums for a life insurance policy. At the end of the period agreed when you took the loan, the mortgage loan is repaid from the proceeds of the life insurance, and any extra is yours.

While with most endowment policies you get the best return by making payments for the period originally agreed, it is possible to stop paying earlier. You have two options. The first is to 'cash in' the policy. The amount you get is up to the insurance company (but if you are cashing in a policy within ten years of having started to pay the premiums you will owe tax). The other option is to make the policy 'paid-up'. You stop paying premiums and the insurance company reduces the amount of money they guarantee to pay out when the policy comes to an end.

Ask whether bonuses will continue to be paid on a paid-up policy. The company will be able to tell you the cash-in and paid-up value of your endowment policy. You should also find out what the current sum guaranteed by the policy is if you continue with it to the end of its term. The chances are that the sum guaranteed is very much higher than the paid-up value which, in turn, is even higher than the cash-in value.

Unless you are desperate to pay off the mortgage loan and the cash-in value is high enough to do this, it is almost certainly not worth cashing in the policy.

It is only possible to make it paid-up if the current paid-up value is high enough to pay off your loan or if you are able to pay off the mortgage from another source. Alternatively, if you are moving home you could buy your new home with a repayment (or interest-only mortgage). But it is only worth making the policy paid-up if the insurance company continues to add bonuses.

Continuing to pay the insurance premiums may well be the best choice because you certainly get the best return from a with-profits endowment policy if you continue paying premiums for the period originally agreed.

if you have a repayment mortgage

With a repayment mortgage, each instalment you pay reduces the amount you owe the lender. In the early years, only a very small amount of your payments are capital – in the first year you may repay only around one percent of the total amount borrowed – but this rises over the years until the final year, when almost the whole of your payments are used for repaying the loan.

If you are trying to decide whether or not to pay off a repayment loan, the problem is how to work out the actual interest rate you are paying. This is particularly difficult with many lenders (including most of the building societies) because they base the amount of interest you have to pay each year on the amount you owe at the start of the year, even though you pay off part of the loan each month.

This means that the effective rate of interest you are paying is higher than that quoted because the amount of money you owe for eleven out of twelve months is less than the amount on which you are paying interest.

Even in the first year of a mortgage, the effective rate of interest is higher than the quoted figure – for a mortgage at 13% the actual interest rate is around 13.85% (10.4% after tax relief) – but it is only in the last couple of years that the rate rises by a significant amount.

TRUE INTEREST RATES ON A REPAYMENT MORTGAGE
AFTER TAX RELIEF AT 25%

years left for *mortgage to run*	*interest rate quoted by lender*				
	10%	11%	12%	13%	14%
	%	%	%	%	%
25	7.9	8.7	9.5	10.4	11.2
20	7.9	8.7	9.6	10.4	11.2
15	8.0	8.8	9.6	10.5	11.3
10	8.1	8.9	9.8	10.6	11.5
5	8.5	9.4	10.3	11.2	12.1
4	8.7	9.6	10.6	11.5	12.4
3	9.2	10.1	11.1	12.0	13.0
2	10.1	11.2	12.2	13.3	14.4
1	14.6	16.2	17.8	19.4	21.0

Applying the principle outlined earlier that it is only worth paying off the mortgage if the interest you pay on the loan is higher than the interest you can get by investing money, it is likely that you should consider paying off your mortgage in its last couple of years – assuming that your lender used this method of calculating interest. Some lenders recalculate interest each month and this advice would not apply then. Ask your lenders what method of interest calculation is used and also ask them to work out for you the interest rate you are actually paying.

other points to consider before paying off your mortgage

○ Will you have to pay a fee for paying off your mortgage early? Most of the large building societies and banks do not charge a fee to borrowers who want to pay off their mortgage early. Some of the smaller societies and banks and insurance companies do charge a fee which can be as much as three months' interest. Some will accept three months' notice instead. So do check this before making a decision.

○ If you decide not to pay off your mortgage (or pay off only enough to bring the total loan down to £30,000 in order to make the most of tax relief), invest any remaining lump sum wisely. (The chapter on Investments , in this book, will help you do this. You may also find it useful to read *Which? Way to Save and Invest*.)

moving

If you decide that you need a different house, and will want to move, plan as far ahead as you can and do some thinking and researching.

The points you should consider include

○ the size and value of your home now as against the size and value of the home you will need when you retire
○ what you can buy elsewhere with the proceeds of selling the present home
○ the cost of moving
○ the income from investing any surplus lump sum, if what you get from selling is more than you need for buying
○ the saving you could make in running costs by moving to a smaller house (rates, heating, maintenance); conversely, the increase if you move to a larger one
○ the savings you may be able to make by living in a cheaper area (and vice versa).

If you think that it will make sense to move, get some idea of the value of your present home (estate agents will give you a free estimate of what your home might sell for if they were to sell it) and also what you might have to pay for the kind of house or flat you want. Then make some estimate of the cost of moving (which may be up to 10% or so of the value of your new house). If you are worried that your income will be too low when you retire and you need or want more money, you can 'trade down' – that is, buy cheaper than the house you are selling (smaller, or in a less expensive area) and get a lump sum. You can then work out how much will be left for you to invest as a result of your move, to give you more income.

If you decide to move, one advantage of doing so straight-away is that there may be a lump sum from your pension to spend on a house (which may be vital if you have been living in rented accommodation and are an elderly first-time buyer). A person who is approaching retirement age, or has passed it, may not be able to get a mortgage from a building society easily and might have to find some other lender. An older borrower may have to provide additional security or to pay higher interest rates for a short-term loan.

moving more than once?

It is worth considering whether it is better to make only one move to a house or flat which will be suitable for the remainder of your life, or whether it is advisable to plan for two phases – the active and the older, less active – and risk the unsettling effect of a second move at a later time when it may be less easy for you to adjust.

Difficult though it may be, try to anticipate your needs and attitudes ten, twenty or even more years from now. If there are two of you, consider also what kind of home would be suitable for your widow/widower living there alone. A frequent trigger of a decision to sell up and move is bereavement, but if your partner dies you would probably be well advised not to make a hasty decision about moving.

Ideally, you will want a flat, bungalow or easily maintained house you like, in an area where you will feel safe, in a situation that will sustain you as you become older and less mobile, preferably near family or friends, with shops and transport facilities near, and which will not become too expensive to live in and maintain.

where to move?

Many people think of retiring to the country or to the seaside. However, at a seaside resort, property may cost more than it does where you now live (and food and services may be more expensive, too). Be aware that it is very different living permanently in the middle of the country, or all the year round in a seaside resort, compared with spending a happy two-week holiday there in the height of summer. A holiday resort may be dead in the winter and horribly overcrowded in the summer.

assessing the location

It is a good idea to go and stay in the area you have in mind, wherever it may be, at different times of the year, to try and make an assessment of what living there would be like.

○ How good is the shopping? Is most of what you need, or are likely to want, available in the locality? Are things more expensive than you have been used to? Do this comparison for all that you would need to pay for – not just groceries but also the prices of services such as shoe repairs, and dry cleaners, and cinemas, and afternoon tea in a local shop.
○ Are there any specialist shops of the kind you frequent, such as a health food shop?
○ Is it possible to walk to shops, post office, library, a social centre? Are there facilities for you to carry on with a hobby, an interest, an evening course?
○ What is public transport like; would you have to depend on the car?
○ Does getting about locally mean having to go up and down a hill?
○ How easy would it be to visit friends and relatives, and for them to come to you?
○ Would you be happy, or at least content, to go on living in the area if your spouse or companion died, or would you want to move again?
○ What would happen in times of illness?
○ What is the situation about doctors or a health centre and ancillary services, such as chiropody?

If you are thinking of moving to an area that is popular with retired people, general practitioners are likely to have a high proportion of elderly patients on their lists, and may find it difficult to accept new ones.

In an area with a predominantly ageing population, there may be a strain on the welfare services and more people needing them than there are people able to provide the services. Try to find out, for instance, the length of waiting time for a chiropody appointment or an appointment at a hearing aid clinic.

Only if you decide you like the area in general, and have checked that it is likely to be suitable for you, should you start looking for a particular flat or house.

when to move

You may feel that you would like to live in your new home for a couple of years before you retire, so as to get to know the people and places as a 'working person' rather than a 'retired' one.

However, if you decide to put off a move for, say, two years, you will have the opportunity to find out more about the sort of life you lead when retired, and therefore to have more idea of the district and type of home that will suit you.

If you move immediately on retirement, you start your new retired life in new surroundings. But it may be more convenient to house-hunt and move when you have more free time and are more relaxed for the actual business of putting your present house or flat on the market, finding, viewing and buying a new one, and the whole process of sorting out, getting rid of the accumulated junk of years, packing, and all the worry that goes with a move – even if it is only to a new home three streets away.

On a very practical point, it is easier to move in the spring or summer than in mid-winter. The book *Which? way to buy, sell and move house* deals with the whole subject in great detail.

Buying a second home while you are still working, to move to after retirement, needs the initial capital outlay (and MIRAS does not apply to a 'second home'). But if you can afford it, in the knowledge that you will get a good price when you come to sell your present home, you can start to prepare the second home and gradually adapt and improve it until you are ready to move in. Alternatively, you can let it without having to worry too much about getting the tenants out when you want to move in. Under the Rent Act 1977, one of the cases in which the court must grant an order for possession relates to people who let a house to which they plan to retire. The owner must give the tenant notice in writing on or before the start of the tenancy that he intends to live in the accommodation when he retires from regular employment.

getting a new mortgage

If you are moving to a new home, it could pay you to take out a mortgage, perhaps limiting your borrowing to £30,000 so making full use of the availability of tax relief. If you have a lump sum available which could be used to buy your new home outright, the principle is that it is worth borrowing if the interest charges are less than the interest you can get by investing the lump sum.

What sort of mortgage should you consider? An endowment mortgage is probably out of the question as the life insurance premiums would be very high for someone taking out a new policy who is approaching retirement age. A repayment mortgage would be possible, but the lender may not be prepared to lend for more than fifteen or twenty years; this would make the capital repayments relatively high. A further possibility is an interest-only mortgage.

With an interest-only mortgage, you pay interest on the loan but no capital, and the lender recovers the full amount you borrowed from the value of your house when you move or from your estate when you die. The main advantage of this type of mortgage is that it keeps the costs very low. Obviously, the amount of money your heirs get will be reduced by the amount of the loan (though this reduction in the size of your estate may also reduce the inheritance tax payable on your death).

Interest-only mortgages are becoming increasingly common and many building societies and a few banks and other lenders are prepared to consider lending money on this basis. The main restrictions are on the amount of money you can borrow: most lenders will not lend more than three-quarters of their valuation of the home you want to buy. But this may not be a problem if you are restricting what you borrow to £30,000. Some lenders charge a higher-than-normal rate of interest, so you should check this before deciding on where to go for a loan. You also need to consider the position of your spouse to ensure that he or she will be able to carry on with the mortgage on your death, rather than having to move home or find other assets with which to repay the mortgage loan.

council tenants

A council tenant who does not want to, or is not eligible to, exercise the right to buy and wants to give up a large family size house which has become too big may be able to get it exchanged for more suitable accommodation such as a bungalow or flat.

Some local authorities keep an exchange list of tenants who want to move into council accommodation elsewhere within their area; or two tenants may be able to arrange an exchange independently. It is not easy to move to another authority, but most authorities participate in the National Mobility Scheme and most provide lists of tenants who wish to exchange homes with other tenants within their area and farther away. The National Mobility Scheme is a voluntary scheme agreed between most housing authorities in the UK to help tenants move to a different area if they have a pressing need to move, such as to be near an elderly relative who needs support. Most housing associations also participate. For more details and a nomination for a move under the scheme, go to your own housing authority or housing association.

The Tenants Exchange Scheme has been introduced by the government to help council and housing association tenants to find other tenants in another area with whom they might wish to exchange homes. Unlike the National Mobility Scheme, tenants can register irrespective of what reason they have for wishing to move. It is a do-it-yourself scheme: tenants are expected to look at the lists in their housing department office once a month and contact any tenants with whom they would wish to exchange. Additionally, when you first register, you are matched by the computer with any tenants who it appears would like to swap with you. Permission to exchange has to be requested of the local authorities or housing associations involved. A leaflet about the **National Mobility Scheme** and the **Tenants Exchange Scheme** can be obtained from housing departments or from P.O. Box 110, Gloucester GL1 1PE.

A private nation-wide tenancy exchange scheme for council tenants called **Locatex Bureau** (P.O. Box 1, March, Cambridge PE15 8HJ), can match council tenants who wish to offer or exchange their tenancy with one in another part of the country. Locatex charges a small fee, usually around £10.

A booklet *Wanting to Move?* (no. 12 in the Department of the Environment's series of housing booklets) is available from local councils and citizens advice bureaux. It gives advice to people wanting to rent (including privately) or buy in a new area.

moving to a flat

Moving from a house or bungalow to a flat can be a useful way of both cutting down on expenditure and changing to an environment which is less demanding on your time and energy. Also a flat, with just one front door, may be less vulnerable to theft than a house, particularly a large one. In the winter, you can go away from a flat without having to worry so much about the plumbing freezing.

But, before moving to a flat you need to check exactly what you are letting yourself in for. In particular, you should investigate how the responsibility for maintenance is divided (in the lease) between landlord, tenant and possibly management company. There are no hard and fast rules, and each lease has its own peculiarities.

flats/maisonettes derived from subdividing a house

If a house has been split into two flats, it is likely that the owner of each flat will be responsible for structural repairs and insurance of his part of the building, including the structure. The owner of each flat may have to contribute towards cost of structural work to the other. The greater the number of flats, the greater the likelihood that repairs will be the responsibility of the landlord. In a large house divided into two or three flats only, the maintenance costs per flat will not, on the whole, be significantly different from those for a detached house, and because bills for major works will be shared, there should be a saving on outgoings.

Make sure you have the property thoroughly vetted by a surveyor, who should look at the whole building. As the law stands at present, if a property you want to buy is in need of repairs, it is for you to find this out, not for the seller to warn you.

A frequent cause of aggravation in blocks of flats and in converted houses is noise. So check how well the walls and ceilings keep out noise from outside and from neighbouring flats; look out for wooden (rather than concrete) floors, which on occasions seem to amplify sound and turn an acceptable noise level on one floor into an intrusive and ultimately unbearable din on the floor below. So, if you are looking at a flat, try to imagine the effect of a boisterous family next door or on the next floor.

flats in purpose-built blocks

You can expect that in most blocks all flats are let on identical leases. You may have to undertake to redecorate your flat at certain intervals. The landlord or management company will maintain the building and organise the other services such as lifts; however you will be the one who pays.

questions to ask about service charges

○ What exactly do they cover? You should try to see detailed accounts for the past few years (unless the property is a new one) to see exactly how much is being charged for what services. With a new flat, you can expect the figures to be no more than an estimate – an honest one, you hope – of the likely outgoings.

   Some schemes include the cost of central heating of the whole building and even the cost of providing hot water to all the flats. Given your intended lifestyle, does it warrant this expense? If you intend to spend the winter months away from the flat, for example, will you be happy to be subsidising your neighbours?

○ Is there a sinking fund? If money is put aside year by year to cover major items that recur at long intervals (for example, external redecoration) this should prevent wild fluctuations in the service charge from year to year. Be extra cautious if there is no sinking fund, but in any event make detailed enquiries about anticipated future expenditure.

o What major items of machinery could go wrong? Lifts and boilers and central heating systems are not cheap items to repair, usually horrifyingly expensive to replace. Check what, if anything, is covered by insurance.

o To what extent are tenants involved in management? Sometimes management companies are owned and run by the tenants, which means that everyone's voice can be heard. Blocks of flats whose management is in the hands of the tenants can sometimes achieve remarkable economies in overheads. (It is often the retired tenants who are able to take on much of the administrative burden.)

With larger blocks, it is usual for professional managing agents to be employed (by the landlord or management company, as appropriate). These should have the expertise and resources to tackle the job efficiently, but must, of course, be paid for their trouble.

o Are the existing tenants happy with the way the block is run? Try to ask several tenants, to get a cross-section of opinion; but you must expect to find at least one disgruntled customer even in the best run schemes.

A landlord has a vested interest in ensuring his tenants' satisfaction. If he is responsible for maintenance and ignores their problems, they may be able to force him to sell the freehold to them, and at the very least they can consider withholding rent. If there is a management company to undertake the legal responsibility for maintenance laid down in the lease, but it is not owned by the tenants, it means that the landlord has passed the buck so far as maintenance is concerned. You will need to check that the company is reputable and properly run. Ask what other flat schemes it runs, and try to visit one.

If there is a tenants' association, ask whether it is one that is 'recognised' by the landlord and whether its wishes are heeded.

The Consumer Publication *Buying, owning and selling a flat* deals in detail with all these matters.

sheltered housing

Private sector sheltered housing, also called retirement homes or homes for the elderly, usually consists of developments of living units sold on long leases to people who satisfy a minimum age requirement, perhaps 55 or 60. These units may be houses, bungalows or flats. Such developments employ a resident manager, sometimes called a warden, whose job is to act as a 'professional good neighbour'. Each unit can be expected to be provided with an emergency alarm system, and to be designed (to a greater or lesser extent) with the requirements of older people in mind. But they are meant for people still well enough to be able to fend for themselves.

The past decade has witnessed a boom in this market. Developers operating in the provision of sheltered housing range from specialists in the field, through nationally known building firms who have decided that they do not want to be left out of a lucrative market, to small builders and land developers. Town planning authorities generally favour sheltered housing schemes, and may impose less stringent planning requirements on them than on other residential development schemes. So builders can look forward to good profit margins when they enter this field. As the market for sheltered housing is a recent creation, most units currently available for sale are newly built ones. Indeed, because of the relative scarcity of such housing, you could find yourself negotiating to buy a unit where building work has hardly begun.

Units within sheltered housing developments are almost invariably sold on long leases. The leases are in general outline very similar to leases of normal residential flats, but differ in some important respects. Make sure you understand your legal position on a number of topics.

lower age limit
Find out what the minimum age limit is for residents of the development. It may be that a unit can only be owned by someone who is over 55 to live there himself, or you may be able to buy it an earlier age and sublet it to someone who satisfies the minimum age criterion until you want to live there after your own retirement.

guests
Find out whether you could have, for example, a younger relative staying with you, and for how long. In some developments, guest accommodation can be hired – but would it be available if you needed full-time nursing during an illness?

procedures and fees on resale of the unit
The resale market for the unit is obviously restricted by the requirement of a minimum age of the next occupier of the unit. In some sheltered housing schemes, the landlord has to approve the buyer before the sale can proceed; sometimes the landlord has the right to select the buyer or buy back the unit, either at the current market price or for the amount you originally paid.

There is also a widespread tendency, in the sheltered housing field, for the landlord to charge a fee when a unit is sold. This fee might be $\frac{1}{4}$% or might amount to one percent of the sale price. If a justification for the fee is offered, it will probably be on the basis that the landlord incurs expenses in administration on a change of tenant. One percent may not seem much; rising property prices can, however, make it into a substantial figure. A sought-after development can have a lengthy waiting list of people who want to buy, giving rise to a correspondingly increased selling price, which would compensate for the fee that has to be paid.

Some developments charge a further fee (generally a fixed percentage of the sale price) on sale, as a contribution towards a sinking fund – in other words to cover the costs of substantial items of repair and renewal that will eventually become necessary.

communal facilities
Apart from paying for the upkeep on your unit and other normal outgoings, you will be contributing towards the costs of any communal facilities. Find out just what these will be. Many developments include laundry rooms, some will provide common rooms where the residents can get together and organise functions. Such communal facilities can be vital, as the individual units are often not big enough for entertaining on anything more than a very modest scale. Whether or not you are of a sociable nature, the communal facilities should be investigated thoroughly. Different developments can have a very different approach to this issue.

resident warden/manager
Be under no misapprehensions – his job is not that of a nurse, and he will probably not be providing a round the clock service. But he is supposed to be able to help in an emergency, and to go out of his way to check that residents are well and able to cope with everyday living. Find out during what hours he will be available on site and what cover there is during the hours when he is not there.

rent and rent increases
You can expect the ground rent for a sheltered housing unit to be higher than that for a normal flat. Some leases in ordinary blocks of flats have increasing rent levels. The great majority of leases in sheltered housing schemes provide for regular increases in rent. The good news is that the rent is only increased at intervals of several – perhaps twenty – years, and normally it is linked to the retail prices index to keep track with inflation.

management and service charges
One of the principal aims of sheltered housing is to relieve the individual of many of the burdens of home ownership. Mowing the lawn, finding someone to carry out minor repairs to the house, redecorating – individually these may be minor tasks, but they have to be done day in day out, and collectively can amount to a major responsibility. By buying leasehold sheltered accommodation, the responsibility is passed either to the lessor (landlord) or, more usually, to a management company. Beware of schemes masquerading as sheltered housing but providing an inadequate level of back-up. It is critically important to find out from the start who is managing the development. The 'questions to ask about service charges' for any flat, set out earlier in this chapter, are all relevant in this context.

Although the organisational burdens are being assumed by another body, the financial burden will remain yours, and will be passed on by way of an annual service charge. In a typical development, the service charge might cover items such as

○ maintenance and upkeep of the buildings and common areas including all communal facilities, gardens etc; lighting of hallways and stairways; window cleaning
○ wages of resident manager/warden
○ the maintenance of the resident manager's flat and outgoings on it (rates, telephone)

○ emergency alarm system
○ management and auditing costs.

The costs related to the resident manager are likely to be a large item in relation to the total outgoings. The greater the number of residential units, the more these costs will be watered down by being shared between them.

The charges may be levied annually, quarterly, or even monthly in advance, with a possible adjustment at the end of the year when the final figures are known. To put the actual costs in perspective, sit down and work out just how much it has cost you to run your home hitherto.

Given that many residents in sheltered housing schemes are on fixed incomes, a reputable developer will try to ensure that annual increases in service charges are moderate.

A list of companies offering sheltered housing for sale is available from the **New Homes Marketing Board**, 82 New Cavendish Street, London W1M 8AD (telephone 01-580 5588). Please send a large SAE (with a 20p stamp).

A 30-page booklet, published by Age Concern England and the National Housing and Town Planning Council *A Buyer's Guide to Sheltered Housing* (£1.50 inclusive of postage and packing) is available from the Marketing Department of **Age Concern England**, 60 Pitcairn Road, Mitcham, Surrey CR4 3LL.

residential homes and nursing homes

For people who cannot cope on their own and need someone in full-time attendance, a residential home or nursing home can be an ideal solution. As with most things in life, there are excellent ones and there are awful ones.

A good residential home ought to (but few do) have the feel

of a private hotel, a good nursing home that of a private hospital.

These places are expensive, and can make inroads on savings. However, someone who needs to be there may well qualify for attendance allowance, a tax-free benefit which is not means-tested and can (in conjunction with other benefits such as the state pension) go some way towards meeting the fees.

A book *Residential care – is it for me?* by Rosemary Bland (£2.95) is published by **Age Concern Scotland**, 54A Fountain Bridge, Edinburgh EH3 9PT (telephone 031 228 5656) to help older people who are considering moving into a residential home.

moving abroad

You may think that you would like to live abroad after retirement, perhaps because you have visited a country on holiday and like the way of life there, or because you would like to escape to a warmer, sunnier climate. You should consider all the aspects and implications even more carefully than if you were intending to move to a new area in the UK.

If you have decided to move abroad and know where you want to go, make sure you discover as far as possible what it is like to live there. It might be worth spending a fair bit of time there before you retire to find out what living there permanently really entails – as against being on holiday. Explore the area – visit it at different times of the year, not only during the holiday season or the off-peak season, in either of which the atmosphere and facilities may be atypical. If possible, talk to other British people living in the area and find out their views, and go shopping to see what is readily available, at what prices. Food may be cheap, health care and transport may be expensive, for example. Find out what the public transport system is like – expensive or cheap, reliable or unreliable, frequent or infrequent?

practical aspects

If you do not know it yet, make sure that you will be able to learn the language of the country. Not speaking it would be a great barrier; even so, there is a risk of being isolated, or dependent on an expatriate group. You will probably see less of your family, certainly as far as casual visits are concerned (though they, and others, may want to spend their holidays with you there). If you go and visit them, the fares may be high.

You may think that eventually, when you are very old, you will prefer to be back in Britain and that you should therefore buy a bungalow in Bognor – if only to keep your foothold in the property market. The tax implications of this are very complex. Briefly, if you have accommodation available for your use in the UK, you are regarded as resident for any year in which you visit the UK, and ordinarily resident if you come here most years. The Inland Revenue booklet IR20 *Residents and Non-residents Liability to Tax in the UK* gives details.

Living abroad is likely to involve a completely different lifestyle and therefore different attitude of mind; you should be aware of this before committing yourself to life in another country.

formal aspects

It is important to check pension arrangements in the country where you wish to live. Your state pension can be paid to you, free of UK taxes, in most parts of the world, but you would have to check with your local social security office whether subsequent increases in the pension can be received. Countries where increases are payable at present include all the EC countries, Austria, Bermuda, Canada, Cyprus, Finland, Guernsey, Iceland, Israel, Jamaica, Jersey, Malta, Mauritius, New Zealand, Norway, Sweden, Switzerland, Turkey, USA, Yugoslavia; one notable exception is Australia. If you do not get the increase while you are abroad, you will get the higher rate of pension if you return or visit the UK. If your stay in the UK is only temporary, the lower rate will again be paid when you leave.

Health facilities are most important. See if a health service exists and whether you would be eligible to use it (and, if so, under what conditions). Local health insurance may be available; check whether your British private health insurance, if you have this, covers residence in the country in which you want to live. Try to find out what the standard of medical care is and what, if any, ancillary services there are for the elderly.

It is also vital to investigate local tax regulations; to know whether you need to become a registered resident of the country and what the conditions of doing so are; to make sure you understand your own legal position as a foreign resident. You may need to seek professional advice on these points; in the first place, contact the embassy or consulate of the country where you intend to live, to ask specific questions.

check list

Amongst the things you should find out about are

o health services, availability of drugs
o resident's permit: how, when, for how long, restrictions, cost
o work permit if taking a job, giving (unofficial?) english lessons
o tax abroad – income tax, dual taxation, local taxes (for residents/foreigners)

- tax situation in UK while living abroad, earning, non-earning, short return visits to UK, double taxation relief arrangements
- what happens when there is a change in exchange control regulations: effects on pension payments, effects on dividends, banking arrangements
- the effect on your will
- professional advice abroad
- social security and medical care agreements: see the DSS leaflets for the relevant country, in the SA series, and (for EC countries), SA.29 *Your social security and pension rights in the European Community* and NI38 *Social Security abroad*.

PENSIONS

After retirement, you are likely to have to rely on pensions for your main income. Most people get some benefit, that is payment, from the state; and about half the population can look forward to a pension from an employer's scheme (an occupational pension) as well. Others may have benefits to come from a personal pension scheme, or the older sort of scheme called a 'Section 226 Plan' which was mainly used by the self-employed.

who is eligible for a state pension?

What pension you get from the state when you retire depends on the contributions you will have made to the National Insurance scheme throughout your working life. These could be as an employee, or during self-employment, or by contributing voluntarily.

as an employee

National Insurance contributions have to be paid by employees who earn more than a minimum amount, called the lower earnings limit (LEL), and by their employers. These contributions are deducted by the employer at source and passed on to the DHSS (now the DSS, the Department of Social Security) via the Inland Revenue. The lower earnings limit is set each year by the government (in 1989/90 it is £43 a week). If you earn less than the LEL, you pay no contributions, and earn no pension.

There is an upper earnings limit or UEL (£325 a week in 1989/90), and if you earn more than this, you do not pay contributions on the extra.

For employees on average earnings the rate will be 9% of earnings up to the upper earnings limit.

If you have been 'contracted out' by your employer from the state earnings related scheme (SERPS) you pay a lower rate of contribution on your earnings between the lower and upper limits. The reduction is currently 2% of your earnings and this is known as the 'rebate'.

While you are being paid sickness or invalidity benefit, signing on as unemployed, or receiving invalid care allowance, you are credited with one class 1 contribution for each complete week.

Married women who have been paying the reduced rate contribution (previously the 'small stamp') since before May 1977 are entitled to continue to do so, provided they do not take a break in employment of more than 2 complete tax years in a row. This rate of contribution, however, does not qualify them for a retirement pension (or any NI benefits except those for industrial injuries).

self-employed people

Self-employed people pay a class 2 contribution. This is a flat rate figure (£4.25 a week in 1989/90). It can be paid by sticking special stamps on a card, but more usually today a direct debiting arrangement is made.

If a self-employed person earns more than a minimum figure (£5,050 a year in 1989/90), he or she also pays an earnings-related class 4 contribution. This is collected by the Inland Revenue at the same time as income tax, and is passed on to the DSS.

If you were employed and also self-employed for any period during any year, you will have paid class 2 contributions as well as class 1 contributions. Each of these counts as if it were a class 1 contribution at the lower earnings limit. You therefore gain some additional pension.

voluntary contributions

Class 3 contributions can be paid voluntarily by people want-ing to maintain their National Insurance contribution during periods when they are not being credited. This could include periods studying, or when you were out of the country. They are a flat rate figure (in 1989/90 it is £4.15 a week).

information leaflets

The DSS leaflet NP32 *Your Retirement Pension* (with later amend-ment leaflet) gives full details of contribution requirements and the types of pension. Leaflet NI196 lists the current rates, and there is also a general leaflet FB6 *Retiring? your pension and other benefits*. Leaflet BR19 *How you can get a pension forecast* includes a simple questionnaire.

All DSS leaflets are free, and are available at social security offices, and also some post offices, citizens advice bureaux and local libraries.

DSS records

Each person's National Insurance record is kept by the DSS. At any time before you reach state pension age, you can find out how your contribution record stands by using BR19. You have to give your full name (and any previous name), date of birth, National Insurance number and other personal information. They will work out for you what percentage of the basic state pension your present record will qualify you for. What this will mean in money terms will depend on the current rate of pension being paid when you retire, and on whether you keep up your National Insurance record during the rest of your working life.

The basic rate of pension is increased regularly in line with prices, so the current figure gives you some idea of how much your pension will be worth.

state pension: what you qualify for

The current system of benefits started in 1948, with the Beveridge scheme. The state earnings related pension scheme (SERPS) was added in 1978, and in 1988 further changes were made, cutting back on SERPS for the future and offering new options of personal pensions.

There are three elements to the retirement provision: basic pension, additional (SERPS) component, graduated pension.

basic pension
Provided that you have made enough contributions, the basic pension is paid at a flat rate, regardless of what you have been earning. In 1989/90, the basic pension is £43.50 a week, plus £26.20 for an adult dependent.

additional component, earnings-related
The earnings-related pension from the state is based on earnings between the lower and upper earnings limits throughout the years from April 1978, revalued to take account of inflation.

An employee who is a member of an employer's pension scheme that is contracted out of the state scheme gets a 'guaranteed minimum pension' (GMP), from the employer's scheme, of broadly the same amount as the additional component.

An employee who has been a member of an employer's COMP scheme (explained below on page 60) or bought an 'appropriate personal pension' (explained below on page 61) gets whatever pension has been built up from the contributions that would otherwise have gone into the state earnings related pension, but has no guarantee of their amount.

graduated pension
The graduated scheme existed between 1961 and 1975, and employees paid graduated contributions on a set band of

earnings. They will receive a small extra amount on top of the basic pension, depending on the number of 'units' accumulated. The graduated pension scheme was not inflation-proofed at the time it was in force, which is why the pensions are so small, but since 1978 graduated pensions in payment and waiting to be paid have been increased by the same amounts as the state basic pension.

the basic pension

All classes of National Insurance contributions count towards your basic pension. But employed married women paying the reduced rate of NI contribution have to depend on their husband's contribution record for a pension, at the lower (dependant's) rate.

contributions: how many and how long?

To get any state basic pension you have to meet one of the following conditions. At some point in your working life you must have either actually paid (rather than being credited with) 50 of the flat-rate contributions payable before 6 April 1975 or, since then and up to April 1978, have paid (not been credited with) contributions on at least 50 times the lower earnings limit in a single year. Or after 1978, you must have paid or been credited with contributions, on at least 52 times the lower earnings limit for any one tax year.

In order to get the full basic pension, you must also have done so for a sufficient number of years in your working life. Each year in which you have done so is called a 'qualifying year'. For years before 1975, when there were NI stamps rather than the current system of contributions, you would need to have paid or been credited with 50 stamps for a year to be counted as 'qualifying'.

Any time during which your earnings as an employee were below the lower earnings limit for that year will show a gap in your contribution record, because no contributions will have been deducted from your pay under that level. But when you were drawing certain National Insurance benefits (sickness, maternity, unemployment, etc) you were credited with contributions for those weeks.

You will need to have nearly a quarter of the years in your working life counted as 'qualifying years' to be paid any basic pension at all. To get a full pension, you need to have nine-tenths of your working life counted.

There have been various changes, particularly in the bases for calculating how much pension is paid, since the National Insurance scheme started in 1948. People in different age groups have to qualify in different ways, according to when they started to be in the system. The crucial date is 5 July 1948.

For most people who were over 16 on that date (and so would now be aged 57 or more), the period during which you were expected to have contributed will start from 6 April 1948 – even if at that time you were not working. This period is known as your 'working life'.

Before 1948, the state pension scheme was not compulsory, and allowed entry only to certain groups. If you were one of those who was contributing before 1948, the period during which you will be expected to have contributed starts from the beginning of the tax year in which you started paying into the scheme or, if there was a break in employment, last started contributing.

There are some special provisions to help married women who had started working and contributing before the second world war, and then spent time in the forces or the land army during the war. If they were working and contributing on 5 July 1948, they can use some of their earlier contributions as credits within the scheme. These provisions are complicated and contain a number of anomalies, however. If you think they may apply to you, ask the DSS to check the point, giving whatever details of your employment and forces record before 1948 you can remember.

qualifying years and working life

Years of working life, and 'qualifying years' all start on 6 April in one year, and end on 5 April the next year, just as tax years do. Your working life means the tax years from the year in which you reached the age of 16 to the tax year ending before the year in which you reach state pension age. So a man's 'working life' will be 49 years, and a woman's 44 years. But people coming up to retirement now will have rather shorter 'working lives' in many cases, because the National Insurance scheme started when they were already over 16.

The number of qualifying years normally needed is:

length of working life	*number of qualifying years needed*
10 years	working life minus 1
11–20 years	working life minus 2
21–30 years	working life minus 3
31–40 years	working life minus 4
41 years or more	working life minus 5

There is a table in DHSS leaflet NP32 *Your retirement pension* which shows what percentage pension you get if you fall short of the number of contributions needed for a full pension.

dependants

A man who has dependants when he reaches retirement age, such as a child or a non-earning wife under the age of 60, can claim an increase to his basic pension for the dependants. If his pension is reduced because he has not made enough contributions, the allowance for the dependants will also be reduced. If the wife is earning, the allowance for her will be reduced, or wiped out, if she is earning more than a weekly maximum (currently laid down as £34.70). If she is not living with her husband, the allowance will only be paid if she is earning no more than £26.20, *and* her husband is paying her maintenance of at least that amount.

A woman can get a dependant's allowance for her husband added to her pension, in some rather limited circumstances. For this to apply, she must have been getting an increase in her unemployment, sickness, or invalidity benefit because of him up to the date of her retirement. He must not be getting any state benefit of his own, and must not be earning more than the amount of the increase she would get for him as a dependant.

A parent who reaches retirement age while still drawing child benefit can get an increase in his or her basic pension for the child. This allowance will always be at the standard rate, even if the parent's pension is lower than the full rate.

DSS leaflet NI196 *Social Security benefit rates* gives the current rates for these increases, updated each year.

married women

A married woman who has been paying full-rate National Insurance contributions will be elegible for a pension in her own right, as if she were a single person, provided she has enough qualifying years in her working life. These need not be consecutive, and for many women they will be separated by a number of years during which they were bringing up children.

But if she is not paying full-rate contributions and has continued to pay the reduced rate contribution, she can qualify on her husband's contribution as his dependant. This means that the woman has to wait until her husband retires before she has any entitlement. If she is then under 60, he draws a pension on her behalf as an addition to his own. If she is over 60, it is still at the dependant's rate, three-fifths of the full rate, but it is her own benefit. At the woman's retirement date, the

DSS will check the contribution record and decide how much pension she is entitled to. If that is less than the full amount but more than the dependant's pension on her husband's record, she will get that higher amount. If the pension on her own contributions is less than the dependant's pension, then she will get the dependant's amount.

home responsibilities protection

If for any complete tax year since 1978 you were at home looking after a child, your right to a basic state pension is protected. You are given 'home responsibilities protection' which means that the number of years counted as your working life is reduced, so that it is easier to get together the required number of qualifying years. But you must have at least 20 years in your working life. This protection is given automatically, for any year in which child benefit has been payable and can also apply to a man, not only women.

Home responsibilities protection also covers some people looking after invalids. To get it, you need to have been caring for any elderly or sick relative who was receiving attendance allowance, or receiving income support (formerly supplementary benefit) without being required to sign on as unemployed. You need to apply for this: ask the DSS for a form.

DSS leaflet NP27 *Looking after someone at home; how to protect your pension* gives full details. However, to get HRP you must either have been paying the full rate of National Insurance contribution (not the married women's reduced rate) before you left work, or have committed yourself to pay it. So for a woman who was paying the reduced rate, the sensible thing would have been to commit herself to pay the full rate before leaving work. You do this by filling in the form in leaflet NI1 (or NI51 if you are widowed). You can send in the form at any time during a year, but it takes effect only at the beginning of a tax year, in April.

divorce or death of your spouse

A widow or a divorced woman can use her late or ex-husband's National Insurance contribution record for the years of the marriage, to fill any gaps in her own record. This is simply a book-keeping exercise, and does not make any difference to his own entitlement. A widower or divorced man has the same right based on the woman's contributions. DSS leaflet NP32A *Your retirement pension if you are widowed or divorced* explains this. However, if you marry again you lose this right, and if you then divorce again, you can only use the second ex-spouse's contribution record for this purpose.

When the husband dies after the age of 65 and the widow is over 60, her retirement pension is changed to the rate of benefit for a widow, which could be higher. On top of this, she will get half of the graduated pension he had been entitled to, and also half of any extra pension he had earned by deferring his retirement.

missed contributions

It is possible to top up your contribution record by making voluntary contributions to fill in recent gaps, and this may be worth checking if you take early retirement, for instance.

You can ask the DSS to give you details of your National Insurance record, and for how long you missed paying. You may find that you have missed contributions for reasons that mean you do not have credits. The most common of these is that before 1978, women who took time away from paid work were not given any protection for their pension.

If there are recent gaps, you can make up by paying class 3 contributions any time up to the end of the 6th year after the year in which you had missed making contributions. DSS leaflet NI48 *Unpaid and late paid contributions* gives details of when you can make back payments of contributions, and leaflet NI42 explains about voluntary contributions.

earnings-related (additional) pension

On top of the basic state pension, there has been, since 1978, a state earnings related pension scheme (known as SERPS). If you are an employee and have made no other pension provision, you are automatically a member of this. This means that you get a pension from the state linked to your earnings. If, however, you have been in an employer's scheme which is contracted out of the state scheme, or in one of the new contracted-out personal pension provisions, you do not get SERPS for those years. How this works is explained below. Self-employed people do not belong to SERPS.

What additional pension you get under SERPS depends on the level of earnings on which you have been paying class 1 contributions over the years. You can be paid SERPS for odd years, so even if you do not qualify for the basic state pension because of its contribution conditions, you may qualify for some SERPS pension.

A married woman who has been paying full National Insurance contributions will get SERPS based on her earnings in her own right, even if she is relying for her basic pension on her husband's contribution record.

The government is phasing down the amount available from SERPS, from the beginning of the next century. However, the amounts earned between 1978 and 1988 are to be safeguarded.

What you get as an additional pension will depend on

○ the date at which you reach state retirement age
○ your earnings in the years between 1978 and that date
○ the increase in average earnings in the country as a whole during those years, as measured by an index published by the Department of Employment.

To calculate what you are entitled to, the DSS take the earnings between the lower earnings limit and the upper earnings limit (currently £43 and £325 a week respectively) for each tax year since 1978/79. They then uprate these figures by the increase in national average earnings since the date you earned the money. Then if you are retiring before 1999/2000, they give you $\frac{1}{80}$th of those 'revalued average earnings' for each complete tax year since 1978/79. So, for instance, if you are retiring in 1989/90, you would have 10 complete tax years in the scheme and would get $\frac{10}{80}$ths.

The most anyone will be able to get is $\frac{20}{80}$ths, and after the turn of the century the scheme will be phased down.

You can find out an estimate of your SERPS entitlement from the DSS. Get leaflet BR19 from your local DSS office, fill in the form and send it to Newcastle. The information you will get includes
○ the amount of SERPS additional pension you can expect to get based on the National Insurance you have paid so far
○ an estimate of what the SERPS pension will be if you carry on working until normal state pension age and your future earnings go up at the rate of inflation, and if they increase faster than inflation.

This is a set of guesses, but it will be useful for giving you some idea of what you will have from the state.

A widow will get part of her husband's additional pension from SERPS, even if the husband dies before state retirement age; a widower who is over 65 at the time of his wife's death gets part of her additional pension if she is over 60 when she dies. Up until April 2000, this can be up to the full amount of the deceased spouse's entitlement, so long as this, added to the widow/er's own SERPS, does not give more than the maximum additional pension that a single person could have had from SERPS. If the spouse dies after 6 April 2000, however, the widower or widow will inherit only half the deceased's SERPS pension.

if you are contracted out

You can be contracted out of the SERPS scheme and obtain your pension from another source, either via your employer or via your own personal scheme. There are now two different ways of contracting out. One is related to your earnings; the other is 'money purchase'.

contracted out salary related (COSR) schemes

Most large employers, and many smaller ones, have schemes of this sort. You pay lower National Insurance contributions to the state, and a 'rebate' of 2% of your earnings above the lower earnings limit is expected to go into the employer's scheme to pay for the guarantees it has to give. The employer also receives a rebate, of 3.8%. The guarantees are that the scheme will give benefits equal, in most cases, to those that you would otherwise have had from SERPS. In any case where there is a shortfall, the state contracts to make up the difference. This SERPS-equivalent pension is referred to as the guaranteed minimum pension or GMP. Once it is being paid, the state increases most of it in line with any general increase in prices. (For GMP that has built up after April 1988, the scheme itself must pay an increase of 3% a year, and the state only makes up the difference between that and the rate of inflation.)

contracted out money purchase (COMP) schemes

Since April 1988, it has been possible for an employer to contract people out in a different way, by guaranteeing to pay into the scheme at least as much as the National Insurance rebate on the employer's and employee's contribution. There is no guarantee of the amount of benefit that will be paid at the person's retirement. This will depend entirely on the investment returns and annuity rates available. The guaranteed contributions create what are called 'protected rights', with special conditions attached. You replace your SERPS additional pension for these years with the protected rights pension, which may be more or less than SERPS would have been. After retirement, the 'protected rights' pension must increase by 3% a year compound. The state gives increases on its SERPS element, with a 3% offset for a notional amount for each year during which you have been contracted out.

personal pension
Since July 1988, it has also been possible to contract out of SERPS as an individual, by taking out an 'appropriate personal pension' (APP). This can be provided by a bank, a building society, an insurance company or a unit trust. The DSS acts as a clearing house for contributions to these, and pays over the National Insurance rebate for both employer and employee to the personal pension provider. This money goes to create 'protected rights' to a pension at state retirement age, based on the investment returns to the fund and the annuity rates currently available. There are no guarantees of the amount, and when you contract to take out a personal pension, you give up your SERPS pension for those years.

With both a personal pension and a COMP, much depends on the age at which you make the contributions. The older you are, the less likely it is that the investment returns can give a higher pension than you would have had from SERPS. Certainly, anyone with less than twenty years to go before retirement would probably be unwise to contemplate contracting out of SERPS by this method.

graduated pension

Between April 1961 and April 1975, the government ran a 'graduated pension' scheme. All employees either paid into this, or were 'contracted out' by their employers into similar schemes. Anyone who paid graduated contributions during this time gets extra pension per week from those contributions.

how much?

The pension comes as pence per 'unit' of graduated contributions. For a man, the unit is £7.50, for a woman it is £9. The unit was originally fixed at an old 6d (2.5p) but since 1978 it has increased each time the state pension increased. Anyone retiring in 1988/89 will get 5p per unit.

When the graduated scheme ended in 1975, everyone who contributed was sent a statement of how much they had paid in, and how many units they had accumulated. By multiplying the number of units to your credit by the current value of the units, you can work out how much you will get as graduated pension. It will never be very much, however, as what originally looked like a reasonable pension was eroded by inflation for every year up to 1978, when it started to be inflation-proofed.

How you can get a Pension Forecast (leaflet BR19) can also be used to find out how many units you have and what they are worth.

A married woman who has earned her own graduated pension can claim this when she reaches 60 and retires, even if she is not then getting the basic pension – for instance, because she is relying on her husband's contribution record for this and he has not yet retired. A widow or widower can inherit half the late spouse's graduated pension entitlement to add to her or his own, regardless of his or her own eligibility. But the amount of graduated pension he or she receives in all must not be more than the maximum a single person would get.

retiring earlier

You cannot draw state pension before state retirement age, even if you want to (or have to) give up paid work before then. If your early retirement is brought about by ill-health, you may well find you qualify for state sickness benefit and invalidity benefit meanwhile.

If you want to retire before state pension age, ask your local social security office to check whether your NI record, up to the date you plan to retire, is enough to provide a full basic pension when you reach the qualifying age. If not, it might be worth making voluntary class 3 contributions during the intervening years, to make your record as complete as possible. Contributions can be made up to the end of the tax year which includes your qualifying birthday (65th for a man, 60th for a woman).

unemployed before retirement

A man who becomes unemployed between the ages of 60 and 65 is credited with National Insurance contributions, even if he is not drawing unemployment benefit, for any time during the period from the start of the tax year before his 60th birthday, to the end of the one before his 65th birthday. So his pension when he reaches 65 will be calculated as if he had been making contributions during those years.

A man or woman under 60, however, does not get credits during unemployment in the same way. They can – and if necessary, should – make up their contribution record by paying voluntary contributions, or sign on as unemployed and receive automatic credits.

the £35 rule

For anyone retiring over the age of 55, who has a pension from an employer, or a personal pension, of over £35 a week, any unemployment benefit received is reduced £ for £ above that amount. So, for instance, if you have an occupational pension of £40 a week, you will lose £5 a week of unemployment benefit. Unemployment benefit lasts a year; after that, if you do not have enough to live on, you may be able to claim income support.

retiring later

You should get your right to a pension established at state pension age. The DSS can tell you then what is payable to you, including any graduated or earnings-related additions.

You can, however, defer your retirement. A few months before you reach state pension age, the DSS will send you a form. One of the questions on this is "Do you intend to retire?". Putting the answer "No" means that payment of the state pension will be postponed until either you do retire, or you reach the age of 65 for a woman, 70 for a man. Above those ages, the state pension is paid whether you have retired or not.

Your eventual pension will increase by 1% for every seven weeks that you work beyond state pension age (after the first seven weeks). So if you continue to work for the full five years, you will have a pension of about one-third more. For any weeks when you are unemployed or sick, you will receive National Insurance benefits at the same rate as the state pension, but you will not be given increases on your state pension for those weeks.

If a pension is deferred, any benefit payable for a dependent wife must also be deferred. It can only be drawn when the husband himself retires, but it is then similarly increased.

If you go on earning over pensionable age, you do not have to pay National Insurance contributions, although the employer has to continue to do so for 5 years beyond your state retirement age.

change of mind

After you have retired, you may want to return to reasonably well-paid work. You can 'cancel' your retirement by notifying the DSS, and the pension will be held for you and increased in the same way as an initially deferred pension is. However, for a married man whose wife is receiving a pension based on his contribution record she has to agree to his cancelling retirement, because it would mean loss of her rights also. If she agrees she must sign the form (BR432) on which he notifies the DSS of the cancellation. Her pension, when resumed, will also be increased.

You can only cancel your retirement once. Thereafter, when you have re-retired, you cannot cancel again.

DSS leaflet NI92 deals with the cancellation of retirement.

carry on working

Some people will wish to carry on with paid work after state retirement date. You may be able to do this, and still draw your pension. You are generally counted as 'retired' for pension purposes if

- ○ you do not do any paid work at all; or
- ○ you do not work for more than 12 hours a week; or
- ○ you work only occasionally.

earning while retired

Once you are getting a state pension, your earnings are covered by the 'earnings rule'. This means that if your earnings, after deductions for reasonable work expenses, come to more than a set maximum each week, the basic state pension you are getting is reduced. For 1989/90, the earnings limit is £75 a week. The reduction is 5p for every 10p of earnings between £75 and £79 and 5p for every 5p above that. Once a man reaches the age of 70 and a woman the age of 65, however, no deduction is made regardless of how much they earn.

The earnings related additional pension and the graduated pension, however, are not affected by the earnings rule. Nor are amounts by which the basic pension has been increased because of deferred retirement.

It is up to you to tell the local social security office if your earnings in any week (from sunday to the next saturday) exceed the earnings limit. Leaflet NP32 explains what counts as earnings, and what does not have to be included.

getting the pension

About four months before you reach state pension age, the DSS normally sends you a claim form. Fill this in and return it to your local social security office. If you have not received a form by three months before your birthday, ask your local social security office about it. If you do not do this, or do not fill in the form, your pension will be delayed and you may lose some of the arrears.

how much?
In due course, you will be sent a statement of what pension you are entitled to, and how this is made up. If you are due to get a 'guaranteed minimum pension' (GMP) from an employer's contracted out pension scheme, the statement will tell you the name and address of the person or company responsible for paying you this. You will also be told what you need to do if you disagree with the decision about your pension payment, and want to challenge the calculation.

A wife who is claiming a pension on the basis of her husband's contribution record must give notice of her retirement date and complete the claim form within 3 months of that date.

You must make a separate claim for an increase in your pension because of a dependant. Do this at the same time as you make your own claim. In any case you must do so within 3 months of the date you become eligible for the pension. Otherwise you may lose some of the benefits.

deferred retirement

If you are deferring your retirement, state this on the form and return it. You will then be told what pension is due to you. Later on, when you do decide to retire, notify the local social security office about 4 months in advance, or as soon as possible. It is not usually possible for a pension to be backdated further than 3 months.

how it is paid

The pension is payable on a weekly basis, in advance, by orders cashable at a post office. You have to specify which post office. If you want to change the branch at which you are drawing it, you must notify the DSS.

Pensions are generally paid on mondays, but you do not have to collect the pension every monday. You must, however, cash an order within 3 months of the date shown on it.

Alternatively, you can elect to have the pension paid directly into your bank account or National Girobank or National Savings Bank investment account, or into a building society account. When the pension is paid in this way (called 'credit transfer') it is paid either 4-weekly or quarterly in arrears. If you want to receive your pension by credit transfer, ask for form NI105 and complete the application form in it.

It is possible to arrange to be sent a girocheque every quarter, so that you can pay it yourself into any account that you hold.

You will not get any pension until the first monday after your date of retirement. The first pension payments that you get may turn out to be less than the full amount due to you, while the exact amount is being calculated. Any arrears will be paid to you as soon as these calculations are complete.

if you go abroad

You can generally get your retirement pension anywhere abroad. If you are going abroad for less than 3 months, you can normally let the pension build up and cash the orders when you return. But remember that a pension order can only be cashed in the 3 months after the date shown on it.

If you are going abroad for longer than 3 months, tell the social security office in plenty of time before you go, so that they can make arrangements to have your pension paid abroad.

Check also whether Britain has a 'reciprocal agreement' with the country to which you are going. Only in countries with such an agreement will you have the benefit of any pension increases. In countries without one, you are paid only the rate of pension in force at the time when you left the country.

tax and the pension

Your state retirement pension, plus any additions to it except those for a dependent child, is taxable. If you are receiving an occupational pension or are earning, the state pension will be added to these, and tax deducted through the PAYE system. If you have other income which is not taxed via PAYE, you will need to fill in a tax return and pay a lump sum at the end of the tax year.

If the state basic pension is your only income, there will not be any tax to pay.

A married woman who is getting a state pension based on her own contribution record can set her personal tax allowance against this, because the pension counts as her own earnings. But the pension for a married woman based on her husband's contribution record is treated for tax purposes as his earnings, and he must pay tax on this. If the wife could have had a part pension paid on her own contributions, but is receiving one based on her husband's contributions because it is higher, she can have her proportion of it offset against her tax allowance. To do this, write to the tax office setting out the details.

age allowance

From the tax year following your 64th birthday onwards, you receive a tax allowance higher than the usual personal allowance. A married couple qualifies when one of them reaches the 64th birthday.

The amounts change each year with the Budget. For the 1988/89 tax year, the age allowance is £3,180 for a single person, or £5,035 for a couple.

But for every £3 by which your 'total income' exceeds a set amount (£10,600 in 1988/89) you lose £2 of the age allowance. So when a single person's income reaches £11,462 or a married couple's £12,010, the age allowance has been wiped out, and the normal personal allowances apply instead. In 1988/89 this is £2,605 for a single person, £4,095 for a married couple.

'Total income' for this purpose means gross income, minus any interest payments which qualify for tax relief. These might be mortgage payments, or payments on a loan for home improvements taken out before April 1988, or payments to a personal pension fund, or under a covenant.

Inland Revenue leaflet IR4, available free at tax offices, explains about income tax and pensioners; leaflet IR4A deals with the age allowance.

a pension from your job

The amount of pension and other benefits that an employer's approved pension scheme can pay is limited by the Inland Revenue. A pension scheme does not qualify for tax relief under the Finance Act 1970 unless it is approved. As these tax reliefs are valuable, in practice it means that the Inland Revenue limits are the maximum for all pension schemes run by employers.

For most schemes, these limits are

○ the maximum pension you can get at the scheme's normal retirement age is two thirds of your total final remuneration, provided you have been at least 20 years with the employer;
○ part of what you get may be taken as a tax-free lump sum. This must not be more than $1\frac{1}{2}$ times your final remuneration, or £150,000, whichever is the less. If you were in the pension scheme before 17 March 1987, you are allowed this maximum lump sum after 20 years' membership. For anyone who joined after that date, the rules are more complicated and, in most cases, mean that the maximum will only be reached after 40 years' membership;
○ a pension which is being paid out can be increased either by a fixed amount, or by the amount needed to keep it up with the retail prices index;
○ the maximum total contribution an employee may pay in any one year is 15% of his or her remuneration in that year, with full tax relief on it. There is no limit on the size of the employer's contribution.

Schemes tend not to be as generous as the Inland Revenue would allow; one that would pay benefits to that limit would be costly for the employer to provide.

the exception: a COMP scheme
Contracted Out Money Purchase schemes can choose whether

to stick to these limits, or instead to curb the amount that is put in. If they do the latter, the maximum contribution available, from employer and employee together, is $17\frac{1}{2}\%$ of earnings. There is still a limit of £150,000 on the lump sum, which must not be more than a quarter of the total fund that is built up for the scheme member.

Few COMP schemes have followed these rules; in most cases they are taking the 'maximum benefits' route instead, as it is less restrictive.

the pension you may get

There are a number of different ways in which the pension can be worked out. The main ones, however, are 'final earnings' and 'money purchase' schemes. Some employers operate a belt-and-braces approach, providing benefits based on whichever calculation gives the higher amount. These are often called hybrid schemes, or described as having a money purchase underpin. A few schemes are based on your average pay throughout your working life, or provide a fixed sum for each year of membership, these will generally offer a very poor pension.

Whatever your scheme, ask the pensions manager, a few months in advance of your retirement date, what pension you will be receiving. You have a right to be given details of your benefits on request, once a year. Many schemes in fact give automatic statements of benefits annually, and it will be helpful to keep these in the years approaching retirement.

final earnings schemes

In a final earnings scheme, the pension depends on your earnings near retirement, the number of years that you have belonged to the scheme, and the accrual rate. This is the proportion of earnings that you get for each year in the scheme. It may be 1/60th, or 1/80th, or even 1/45th, for each year in the scheme, or it may be put in percentage terms. If you stay with one scheme until retirement, your eventual pension should have kept pace with increases in your earnings.

The 'final earnings' on which the pension will be based, is on an average figure, perhaps for your earnings in the last few years. It may also not include all your earnings: sometimes, for instance, it is only basic pay, leaving aside such items as bonus or commission; often there is also a deduction to take account of the state basic pension.

Some of the definitions commonly in use are

○ basic pay at the end of the tax year immediately before retirement, or at some other specific date in that last year;
○ the yearly average of total earnings during a specified number of recent years;
○ highest basic pay during the last x years, plus the average of extras such as bonuses, commission, and overtime during a specified period;
○ the yearly average of the best 3 consecutive years' earnings in the last 10 years.

Here is an example of a scheme with an earnings definition of 'annual average earnings over the last 3 years'. Jo Smith is retiring on a final wage of £10,000 a year. She has been earning this for the last year. Before that she earned £9,500 a year, and before that £9,000. Her average earnings over the three-year period, therefore, are £9,500.

When any averaging is done, there will inevitably be a shortfall compared to a formula which allows a single year to be taken into account. This can cause disappointment when someone expects to get a pension based on his or her earnings at retirement.

The pension is then worked out by dividing that final earnings figure by the 'accrual rate', and multiplying it by the number of years in the scheme. So if Jo Smith's accrual rate is a

60th, and she has been 30 years in the scheme, she will receive $\frac{30}{60}$ths of £9,500, which is £4,750.

If the employer's scheme is a contracted out salary related (COSR) scheme, it must provide at least as much as (and usually much more than) you would have had from SERPS. On top of this, you would get the state basic pension, provided you have made enough National Insurance contributions.

money purchase schemes

In a money purchase scheme, the amount of pension you get depends on how much money has been paid in by you and your employers, and how this has built up through the scheme's investments by the time you retire. The younger you were when you started, the longer the contributions have had to accrue interest and dividends, which can themselves be re-invested. It is difficult to build up an adequate money purchase pension for someone who starts paying in at middle age or later, without making very large contributions.

Since different pension providers will be more or less skilful at investment, the amount built up in this way can vary considerably between schemes. In any case, if the investment market in general rises to a peak (as it did in the summer of 1987) or falls into a trough (as in October of the same year), all investors will be affected to much the same extent. The build up of your pension can vary sharply according to the fortunes of the investment market.

The investment of money purchase pensions, unlike final earnings schemes, does not take account of inflation. In times when interest rates are outstripping inflation, as in the last decade, this means that a better pension can be achieved. If inflation were to rise or interest rates to fall in the long term, therefore, the real value of your money purchase pension could be drastically cut, even just before retirement.

The fund that is built up is used to provide you with a

pension, usually through an annuity bought for you from an insurance company. This means that a lump sum is paid to the insurance company in return for the guarantee of a regular income throughout the rest of your life. You have to rely on the trustees of your scheme to select the insurance company, that at the time, will bring you the best annuity.

how much?
The amount of annuity that can be bought with a lump sum is worked out on an actuarial basis. That is, it depends on assumptions about how long a person of your age, sex, and health is likely to live. For the same payment, a woman may receive up to one-third less than a man because of the use of different mortality tables for men and women.

The annuity will depend on interest rates generally, at the time it is taken out. Because of variations in interest rates, different people can get dramatically different pensions for the same level of contributions.

The annuity will not be affected by changes in interest rates after it is bought. It may increase by a fixed percentage each year, or the same size payments may continue throughout the rest of your life.

With a money purchase scheme, it may be possible to arrange to buy an annuity which increases regularly, or to arrange for part of the fund to be held back to pay for increases when the pension is being paid. Either way, the initial pension will be lower than if increases were not going to be paid.

In some money purchase schemes, the pension fund itself provides the pension. An annuity is not bought from an insurance company, but the scheme's trustees assume an annuity rate, generally in line with insurance company rates at the time, and use that to decide how much pension to pay you. The payments are then made straight out of the fund. The rest of the money remains invested and continues to build up income.

contracted out money purchase schemes

With the new COMPS, the fund that has built up as a result of your NI rebate, the employer's NI rebate, and any 'incentive' payments received must be paid at state retirement age and no earlier, and the annuity rate must be the same for men and women of the same age. For a man of 65 and a woman of 60, however, it can still be different and this will mean the woman is getting a lower pension at state retirement date than a man who has paid in the same amount in contributions.

This 'protected rights pension' must be increased by 3% a year compound, or the increase in the retail prices index, if lower.

effect of the state pension

Many occupational pension schemes take account of the pension you will be getting from the state, when calculating the pension they will pay you. For example, the amount of the single person's basic state pension may be deducted as part of the calculations of what are your pensionable earnings. Your contributions to the employer's scheme will probably also have been based on earnings which ignore a first 'slice' of your earnings, roughly equal to the amount of the single person's state pension. This is often described as 'integration' with the state scheme.

In some schemes which are contracted-in to the state scheme, an amount to take account of your SERPS entitlement may also be deducted. This can be done either through a rough-and-ready estimate of your entitlement, or through a more sophisticated – and therefore more complex – calculation.

Integration can make quite a difference to the amount you get. For a lower paid person, an integrated scheme paying $\frac{1}{60}$th of final pensionable earnings will produce less than one providing only $\frac{1}{80}$ but without deduction of the state pension.

lump sum on retirement

With most employers' schemes, you have the option of commuting part of the pension that is due to you into a lump sum
payment. With some schemes, particularly in the public sector,
a lump sum as well as a pension is paid automatically on
retirement.

With most schemes, the pension is reduced if you opt to take
the lump sum. The amount of pension you have to forego
depends on the rules of the particular scheme. It is commmon
for the rules to say that a man of 65 gives up £1 of annual
pension in return for a lump sum of £9; a woman at 60 gives up
£1 in return for a lump sum of £11. The difference between the
amounts for men and women is based on the assumption that
a woman will be living longer and will therefore get her
pension paid for longer.

With some schemes, there is no standard ratio and the actual
amount foregone depends on interest rates at the time you
retire. So you cannot calculate accurately in advance how
much pension you will lose in order to get the lump sum you
would like on retirement.

You do not have to pay tax on any lump sum that is part of a
pension package, but the Inland Revenue restrict the size of
the lump sum in all schemes. The maximum depends on how
many years you have worked for the employer. At best, you
will be able to have $1\frac{1}{2}$ times your remuneration after 20 years
in the scheme. The maximum amount available is restricted to
£150,000.

The rules of your own scheme may impose other restrictions.
Some schemes still operate under previous Inland Revenue
guidelines, which allowed a quarter of the pension to be
commuted, rather than restricting the amount of cash.

Members of a COMP scheme operating under the contribution based rules (since April 1988) will be able to take a quarter

of the fund that has been built up on their behalf, up to a maximum of £150,000.

If your pension scheme is contracted out of the state scheme, you cannot take a lump sum which would reduce your pension to below the 'guaranteed minimum pension' level, nor below your 'protected rights' in a COMP scheme.

Once the pension has started to be paid, you cannot commute it to a lump sum. However, if you have decided to retire later than the scheme's retirement age, you may be able to draw the lump sum at retirement age, while postponing the pension to a later date. You cannot then have a second lump sum when you do retire.

is a lump sum worth it?

You can invest the lump sum or use it to buy an annuity, and so increase your income in retirement, more than making up for the loss on commuting.

However, check the terms of your scheme to see what you are giving up. Many schemes say that any increases in pension will be related to the pension you are actually receiving, rather than to the original amounts.

Some schemes also relate the widow's or widower's pension to the amount you are actually receiving. You might be giving up a valuable additional right within your pension scheme and, therefore, you need to think carefully before commuting your pension to the full extent allowed.

If the pension you will be getting is inflation-proofed, so that it will be increased in line with the retail prices index, this is such a valuable asset that you should be wary of exchanging any part of it for a lump sum when you retire. But if future increases in your pension are likely to be infrequent and unpredictable, it could be better to exchange as much as possible for a lump sum, which you would invest. If you use at least part of that sum to buy yourself an annuity, this will produce a regular income for the rest of your life.

The whole of the pension from the employer's scheme will be taxable, but only part of the income from an annuity that you have bought from an insurance company is taxed. So you may get a higher net income from your annuity than from the pension.

future increases in your pension

What increases will be made to the pension, in the years after retirement, will depend on the rules of the particular scheme. If you work in the public sector, for instance in the civil service, local government, or the police or fire service, your pension is likely to go up annually by the rate of price inflation during the last 12 months. Very few pension schemes outside the public sector are fully inflation proofed. In cases where nationalised industries have been privatised, often existing scheme members kept their rights to inflation-proofing, but new employees do not have this.

Some schemes guarantee to increase pensions by, say, 3% or 5% compound a year. A few schemes undertake to increase pensions partially in line with inflation each year. They may say, for instance, that they will increase them by two-thirds of the rise in the retail prices index.

It is common, though, for schemes not to guarantee a set increase but to review the position from time to time and to make discretionary increases of varying amounts. With some schemes, these increases are generous so that you are getting close to complete inflation proofing. Your scheme may give a mixture of low fixed increases plus discretionary ones.

These discretionary increases will depend on the financial health of the fund and other demands on it. In some cases, the employer pays for them, and so the amount given will depend on what he can afford. They may disappear if the company is taken over and the new employer takes a different attitude.

future increases with a contracted out scheme
In a contracted out salary related (COSR) scheme, the state will pay full inflation proofing increases on GMP (guaranteed minimum pension) accrued up to 1988. For the GMP accrued since then, the increase will be the retail prices index minus 3%. The employer's scheme will guarantee to pay that 3%.

With a COMP scheme, the scheme will pay the 3%, but the state will pay the extra, on a 'notional amount' which need not be the same as the pension you are actually getting; it is calculated as the SERPS you would have had, if you had not given it up.

making additional contributions

Since April 1988, all employers have had to provide facilities for members of pension schemes to make extra contributions in order to receive extra benefits. These are called 'additional voluntary contributions' or AVC schemes.

You can start making voluntary contributions at any time. The Inland Revenue now allows scheme rules to be flexible, so that you may also stop or suspend your contributions at any time, or vary the amounts paid in. Not all schemes, however, have yet taken advantage of this flexibility.

The most you can pay in contributions, to the main pension scheme and the AVC scheme added together, is 15% of your total taxable pay each year. Thus if your regular contributions are 4% of total pay, you could put another 11% into an AVC scheme.

AVCs have the great advantage that they are paid out of pre-tax income, in the same way as your regular contributions.

Also, the investment returns are not subject to tax. So they can be a tax efficient way of increasing your pension, especially if you are approaching retirement and have not been a member of your employer's scheme long enough to qualify for the full benefits. However, once you have put contributions into an AVC scheme, you cannot get them out until you reach retirement, so they are not a place for your emergency savings.

AVCs are usually on a money purchase basis. Your contributions are invested and build up to provide a fund at retirement. This can then be used to buy extra benefits, within the scheme's rules. You must not, however, go over the Inland Revenue limits. Thus if you would already get a pension of ⅔rds of your earnings, you could buy no more pension – but you could, for example, arrange for a higher fixed rate of pension increase. Some schemes are more flexible than others about the benefits you can have from AVCs, so you should check this out before starting to contribute.

If you were already paying AVCs to your scheme before 7 April 1987, you can take some of the fund built up as a tax free lump sum, subject to the overall Inland Revenue limit explained above. If you only started paying after that date, though, the AVCs must be used to provide pension rather than lump sum. You will still, however, be able to use your AVC pension to replace what you give up from your main scheme in order to buy a lump sum.

In the public sector, you can pay extra contributions to buy extra years of pension. These are called 'added years', and are valuable, especially if you have dependants because they carry rights for them also. This means, however, that 'added years' are also expensive.

The younger you are when you pay in extra contributions, the more they will buy when you retire. But because of the tax advantages, it may well be worth making AVCs even shortly before retirement, rather than putting the equivalent amount into another form of savings.

early retirement

An important point to know is when you can retire and take your pension from the firm's scheme. Most pension schemes fix their retirement dates at the same age as the state scheme, 65 for men and 60 for women. Some, though, have an earlier retirement age for men, while others have a higher retirement age, perhaps 65, for women.

If you retire before the scheme's normal retirement age, your pension is likely to be smaller. The reason is that the pension will probably have to be paid to you for more years than if you retired at normal retirement age, and the contributions and interest that go to make up the fund will have had less time to build up. A pension might be, for example, the amount built up so far, minus 0.5% for each month of early retirement.

In the last few years, however, many schemes have improved their early retirement provisions, so long as you are retiring with the employer's consent. They may say that men can go at any age between 60 and 65 without a penalty, or with only a small reduction. The pension, though, will still only be calculated on the basis of the years you have contributed, so that you lose because you have worked fewer years than you would have if working on till 65.

Normally, if you are retiring due to ill-health no reduction in the pension is made, and in a good scheme there will also be credits for years you could have worked but have not.

In general, the Inland Revenue allow a scheme to pay out on voluntary early retirement, or retirement at the request of the employer, only to people who have reached the age of 50. But a woman can take early retirement from the age of 45 if the scheme's normal retirement age is less than 60 and she is within 10 years of it. The Inland Revenue do not set an age limit on a pension that starts being paid because of ill-health.

If your scheme is contracted out of SERPS, the guaranteed

minimum pension (GMP) can only be paid at state retirement age. Some schemes hold back money, or even prevent people retiring early, to take account of this. Better schemes, however, pay the pension due at the time, and make up any shortfall from state retirement date onward.

As you cannot draw your state pension until you reach state pension age, and are penalised on unemployment benefit, some schemes also include a 'top up pension' to cover the years during which there is a gap in state benefits. Other schemes allow you to take a larger pension to start with, at the cost of a smaller pension later on. In effect, this means that you are gambling on your own life expectancy. If you live only a few years after 65 (60 for a woman), you will have received value for money, but if you live a long time, the permanent reduction in your pension is going to outweigh the earlier temporary increase.

what is the least?
At worst, retiring five years early could reduce your occupational pension by a third.

Check also whether any death benefit continues during early retirement. Only a limited number of schemes do this, but it is a very valuable benefit to keep, especially if your health is poor. Insuring yourself elsewhere at that age could be very expensive.

If you are thinking of retiring early, make sure that you know exactly how the situation is treated in your employer's scheme. Ask for details of the basis on which your early pension will be calculated, so that you know the facts and figures before you make up your mind, and at a time when you can still do something about the pension.

postponing your retirement

If your employer agrees, you may be able to go on working and put off your retirement beyond the normal age. A woman has the right to continue working to the same age as that at which men are compulsorily retired by the employer. If this is 65, then she too can work on to 65.

Usually, your pension is then worked out as if you had retired at the normal time, but will be increased when you do retire to take account of the period for which you postponed retiring. Your contributions will normally also stop when you reach the scheme's normal retirement date.

what is the most?
This increased pension can take you over the normal Inland Revenue limit of two-thirds of total earnings. If you postpone your retirement for five years or more, you can get an amount up to three-quarters of your earnings as a pension.

Within this limit, the amount by which the pension will be increased by postponing retirement depends on the formula used by the particular scheme. The formula takes account of the long-term investment returns and the fact that the pension will have to be paid for a shorter time. A factor of 8% or 9% is common for the rate of increase for each year of deferment.

With other schemes, you continue contributing, and continue also to build up eightieths or sixtieths. The employer is then also continuing to contribute.

In a money purchase scheme, it is unlikely that the employer would make further contributions. Your pension would simply continue to build up in line with investment returns on the fund.

pensions from previous employers' schemes

If you have been a member of a pension scheme under a previous employer, you may have a 'preserved pension' from those years. Write to the trustees of that scheme, or the firm's pension manager or administrator, about four months before you are due to retire. Tell them the date at which you intend to retire, and say that you wish your pension to be paid from then. Ask how much it will be, how it will be paid, what options there are (for instance, to turn part of it into a lump sum) and the tax position.

A preserved pension is usually payable from the normal pension age of the scheme in which it was earned. So you can claim this pension even if you have not yet reached the retirement age of your present employer's scheme. If you retire from your final job earlier than the retirement date of the preserved pension scheme, you may be able to arrange for the preserved pension to start in payment then. It may be at a lower rate, though.

If you work on beyond the normal retirement date of the first scheme, the rules of that scheme will say whether payment can start in any case, or whether it must be deferred to your actual retirement.

just before you retire

How a pension scheme works depends on the trust deed and rules. All members of a scheme have the right to be provided with information about the scheme, including how contributions are calculated, and the benefits. On request, you have a right to details of what your own benefits will be. On retirement, you must be told the amount of benefit to which you are entitled, the conditions of payment, and any provisions for benefit increases.

You should have been given an explanatory booklet about the scheme when you first joined it, and been sent a note about any changes to the rules since then. If you cannot find yours, or think it is out of date, ask for another one. Go through this, and make sure you understand the basis on which your pension scheme entitlement will be worked out, and what other benefits may be available.

About three months before you are due to retire, ask your pension scheme manager for an estimate of what your pension will be, and about the effects of exchanging part of it for a lump sum. Final figures will have to wait until your final pay for that last year is known, but a fairly close estimate can be given by now. Find out also how the pension will be paid and taxed.

Check also what the position is on any dependant's pension on your death. The rules of your scheme are likely to define this, but the trustees may have some discretion, or you may be able to nominate someone as beneficiary.

Some schemes arrange that each person coming up to retirement has an interview with someone in the personnel or pensions department. If your scheme does not do this, ask for an interview for yourself. There are bound to be some points about which you are not clear, and there may be options on which you have to make a decision. It will be useful to prepare in advance a list of all the points you need to know and want to discuss. These could include

- how much your pension will be, both before and after tax
- the basis for the calculation
- how it will be paid, and when; and how soon the first payment will come through after you retire
- if you have been making additional voluntary contributions, how much has built up and what this money can be used for?
- if it is a money purchase scheme, what are the amounts

available to buy an annuity? what are current annuity rates? where is it intended to buy the annuity for you?

○ if you can exchange part of your pension for a lump sum, how large can this be (including any money from AVCs, if you were paying these before April 1987)? by how much will this reduce your pension?

○ whether the pension is guaranteed to be paid for a certain length of time; if you die during that time, is the balance paid as continuing pension, or as a lump sum?

○ if a widow/er's pension is provided, how much will it be? can you arrange for it to be more; if so, how much of your own pension would you have to give up for this?

○ if a widow/er's pension is not automatically provided by the scheme, can you arrange for one? what effect would that have on your own pension?

○ can any dependant other than a spouse get a pension on your death? if so, how much might this be and to whom can it be paid?

○ what increases are likely to be made to your pension once you have retired?

If you are married, it would be sensible to share all the information about your pension arrangements with your husband or wife. Make sure your spouse knows the name and address of the person to notify if you should die first, and what pension should be paid to your widow/er in that case.

calculating how much you will get

If your scheme is based on final pay, you should be told what the scheme's definition of final earnings produces for you.

money purchase scheme
With a money purchase scheme, you may not be told precisely how much is available for buying your annuity, but you should

be given at least an approximate figure both for that, and for how much pension it will produce for you. You should also be told which insurance company, or other source, it will come from. A few pension schemes use their own funds to provide money purchase pensions.

How much the money that has accumulated for you can buy as an annuity depends on the rates available at the time. The pension scheme administrator ought to arrange for you to receive the best rate available, but it you want to check, ask to see competitive quotations from different companies. A poor rate at the time will mean a less good pension for the rest of your life. It is possible, but unlikely, that the scheme rules will allow you to postpone taking a money purchase pension if interest rates are low at the time of your retirement. What you could do is take as large a lump sum as the Inland Revenue allows, invest it temporarily and convert it to an annuity later.

taking a lump sum

Where taking a lump sum is optional, you should be told by how much your pension will be reduced for each £100 you take. Under the Inland Revenue rules, the most a scheme can let you take is $1\frac{1}{2}$ times your final remuneration, in many cases it will be less than this.

Although the lump sum is very attractive because it is tax free, before coming to a decision about it you should bear in mind the effects of future inflation, and the fact that you could be retired for 20 years or more. Consider whether the lower pension will leave you and your family enough to live on, not just in the early years of your retirement but later on. Take into account your likely income from any other sources, such as state pension, investments, or money from a part-time job. An income which seems adequate now could be severely eroded by the effects of inflation over the years.

investing the lump sum

If you take a lump sum, you may be able to invest it to produce a better overall income than the pension you would get from the employer's scheme if your left it intact. But where a scheme's pension is fully inflation-proofed, you are unlikely to be able to invest the sum in a way which will produce a better income. For example, if you exchange £1 of inflation proof pension for £9 of lump sum, you would need a guaranteed return of around 11% above inflation, and before tax, in order not to lose out. If your employer's scheme usually increases pensions in payment by around 3% a year, you would need to be able to invest the lump sum at a return of around 14% before tax in order not to lose out.

The main advantage of taking a cash sum out of your pension lies in the tax benefit. Your lump sum will be tax free, but your pension will be taxed as earned income.

buying an annuity with the lump sum

If you do not expect your pension to be increased much over the years, you could do better by taking the tax free cash and using it to buy an annuity for yourself. The income from an annuity bought by an individual (unlike one bought by a pension scheme on behalf of its members) is treated partly as a return on capital, and partly as interest. Only the interest element is taxable. So, taking a cash sum and buying an annuity would mean that you pay less tax than otherwise.

Once an annuity has been bought, however, the money has gone beyond recall. You cannot later forego the income to get back any remaining capital.

tax on your pension

Your pension from all sources will count as earned income, and will be taxed.

The pension from the employer's scheme should be paid to you with tax deducted through the PAYE system, just as your wages have been. But you may notice that a larger amount of tax than you would expect is taken from the pension payment. This is because your state pension is paid to you in full, without any deduction of tax, and the tax due on it is taken out of your occupational scheme benefit.

If you buy an annuity yourself, the insurance company will notify you how much of the payment is capital, and therefore tax free, and how much is interest, which is taxable. You then need to enter this on your tax return. The insurance company will deduct tax at the basic rate from the interest part of the payment to you. If you are a higher rate taxpayer, you will get a tax demand for the extra tax due. If you are a non-taxpayer, you may be able to arrange for the annuity payment to be made gross. If not, then it is your responsibility to reclaim the tax from the Inland Revenue.

sources of information

There are several organisations which can provide information on various aspects of occupational pensions, including

Company Pensions Information Centre, 7 Old Park Lane, London W1Y 3LJ (telephone 01-493 4757)
They are independent, but are supported by a number of insurance companies. They publish a number of free leaflets for members of pension schemes (send a large stamped addressed envelope with any requests). They can provide informa-

tion generally about occupational pensions, but will not intervene in disputes between individuals and particular pension schemes.

Occupational Pensions Advisory Service, 8a Bloomsbury Square, London WC1A 2LP (telephone 01-831 5511)

OPAS is an independent body, registered as a charity. It has been set up with the object of providing assistance and advice to individuals on all matters relating to occupational pension schemes. They aim to help particularly people with specific problems over the scheme they belong to. OPAS is not an arbitration service, but they can try to clarify the information provided by a scheme to anyone who does not understand or is dissatisfied. They will intervene on an individual's behalf where necessary. There are OPAS advisers in many parts of the country, as well as a central panel of pension experts. They can be contacted either directly or through a local citizens advice bureau.

OPAS advisers do not offer personal financial advice. They can, however, explain the broad implications of the choice to be made under the rules of a particular scheme. There is no charge for their advice and help.

Occupational Pensions Board, Lynwood Road, Thames Ditton, Surrey KT7 0DP (telephone 01-398 4242)

This is a government-established body, mainly to supervise occupational pension schemes, especially those contracted out of the state earnings related pension scheme (SERPS). They publish occasional leaflets on individual rights, and can investigate if it is thought that a scheme is breaking parts of the law with which they are concerned, but they cannot take up individual queries.

Trades Union Congress, Congress House, Great Russell St, London WC1B 2LS (telephone 01-636 4030)

The TUC publishes a *Guide to Occupational Pension Schemes*, and other publications on pensions including a quarterly *Pensions*

Briefing. It can advise and help trade union members with pension problems, either directly or through their own trade unions.

National Association of Pension Funds, 12–18 Grosvenor Gardens, London SW1W 0DH (telephone 01-730 0585)
This is an organisation mainly for trustees and administrators of pension funds. Some of its publications, though, are useful for providing general information about the way pension funds operate.

Association of Pension Lawyers (Ian Pittaway, Secretary, c/o Nicholas Graham & Jones, 19–21 Moorgate, London EC2R 6AU)
Members of this association are particularly concerned with the legal aspects of pension arrangements, and are experienced practitioners in pension cases. A list of the members is available from the Secretary.

Citizens Advice Bureaux may be able to help with preliminary advice on a problem, and will know who you should turn to for more advice. The local branch of **Age Concern** may also be able to help with advice. Addresses of branches are available from Age Concern's information department at Bernard Sunley House, 60 Pitcairn Road, Mitcham, Surrey CR4 3LI (telephone 01-640 5431).

a personally arranged pension

Pension schemes run by employers are now voluntary, and no-one can be made to be a member who does not want to. If you leave your employer's scheme and take no other action, you are automatically a member of the state earnings related scheme (SERPS).

You can then buy yourself a 'personal pension' if you wish. This can be arranged to sit on top of SERPS, so that you obtain both, or you can 'contract out' of SERPS with what is called an 'appropriate personal pension'. In this case, the National Insurance rebate is paid to the providers of the 'appropriate personal pension' instead of into the National Insurance scheme. You then receive a money purchase pension at state retirement date (no earlier) based on whatever these contributions have earned while invested. There are no guarantees about the amount you will get.

The younger you are when starting, the longer the money invested has to build up, and the more it will therefore increase. Conversely, the older you are, the less time it has to build up.

For a man in his forties, or a woman in her late thirties, to take out an 'appropriate personal pension' would not be wise, and the older you are, the less wise it is.

It is very unlikely that you can do better by taking out a 'personal pension' than by staying in your company scheme, even if you put a considerable amount of money into it. The major fault in company schemes tends to be their treatment of early leavers, but by the time you reach your 50's you are unlikely to move on elsewhere of your own accord, and if the employers ask you to go they may well offer generous early retirement provisions.

The more reputable insurance companies are refusing to sell personal pensions to people who are in a reasonable company scheme. Even those in poor schemes are generally going to do better by staying within them and paying extra contributions, than by going outside.

Since this book is addressed to older people, the rest of this chapter is going to assume that you have taken out a personal pension because you could not join an employer's scheme, and that you have not contracted out of SERPS, but are keeping your pension on top of it.

self-employed people

A self-employed person has always had the right to participation in a personal pension scheme, under the old legislation which authorised what were called 'Section 226' schemes, and under the new arrangements.

Self-employed people are not paying into SERPS, and therefore will receive only the basic state pension. In order to give themselves a comfortable retirement, therefore, they need to pay for a personal pension. The earlier you start to do this, the better, but even if you start very late in life, paying in the maximum will be worthwhile – if only because it is tax-efficient.

employees without a pension scheme

If your employer does not have a pension scheme, then you are automatically in SERPS unless you opt out into an 'appropriate personal pension'. Alternatively (and more wisely for an older person), you can put a personal pension on top of SERPS. You may be able to persuade your employer to add contributions to your own; there is, however, an overall limit on the amount that can be put in.

The same applies if you have a main job with a pension scheme, but a second job without one. From your earnings from the second job you can make contributions to a personal pension scheme if you want to.

what are personal pensions?

Personal pension schemes are basically savings plans or policies run by insurance companies, banks, building societies and unit trusts. They must be approved under the Financial Services Act, and also by the Occupational Pensions Board if they are running appropriate (contracted out) personal pensions. You pay premiums, either regularly or in lump sums at intervals, to the organisation which invests the money. When you retire, the organisation uses the invested money to provide you with a pension until you die. Part of the accumulated money can usually be taken as a tax-free lump sum when you retire.

Once you have put your money in one of these schemes, you cannot usually get at your money until you retire.

All these personal pension plans are money purchase; that is, what you get is related to the investment returns on your contributions, and not to your earnings at retirement. This means that while these plans can do very well if the money is carefully invested, they can also do very badly, and they can be severely eroded by inflation.

the new arrangements for personal pensions

Until July 1, 1988, personal pension schemes had to be approved by the Inland Revenue under Section 226 of the relevant Finance Act and had to follow certain rules. For policies bought after July 1, 1988, however, the rules changed. The new arrangements are modelled on the old ones, but with various differences.

If you already had a Section 226 policy in existence before 1 July 1988 (not in paid-up form), you can normally continue to pay into it for as long as you wish. But if you want to start a new policy today, it has to be under the new rules.

Section 226 policies ('retirement annuity contracts')

There is a maximum that can be contributed to one of these policies. It is 17.5% of annual earnings for anyone born after 1934, more if you were born before 1934 (namely 20% of earnings for anyone born between 1916 and 1934). Your employer is not allowed to contribute any part of this.

The contributions have to go to an insurance company. They are then invested, and the fund builds up free of income tax or capital gains tax until you reach your retirement date. You have to specify a retirement date at the time when you take out the policy, and in most cases (except for specific professions where it is lower) this cannot be less than 60. The fund that has built up is then used to provide an annuity at your retirement. The policy can also provide limited death benefits, and you are entitled to take some of the fund as a tax-free lump sum, which must not be more than three times the pension that is left.

The rules for personal pensions

For a personal pension, you can put in 17.5% of your earnings if you under 50, or more if you are older (20% if aged 51–55; for someone between 56 and 61 years it is 22.5%; the maximum, for someone over 61 years, is 27.5%). You must specify a retirement age when you start the policy; this can be any age between 50 and 75. Up to 5% of your contributions can be used to provide a lump sum death benefit. The employer is allowed to add contributions also, so long as they do not go above the overall 17.5% (or higher) limit.

At retirement, a quarter of the fund can be taken as cash, up to a limit of £150,000 for each personal pension policy held. This rule differs from that for Section 226 policies, and normally means a rather lower amount of lump sum than was available under the old rules.

Any money held in an 'appropriate personal pension scheme' (that is, contracted out) has to be taken as pension and not as lump sum. There are also various other restrictions on this.

types of pension plan

How the pension you get from the money invested in a pension plan will be worked out, depends on the type of plan as well as on the insurance company, bank, building society or other organisation you have invested with. The two main methods of calculating the pension are deferred annuity and cash-funded.

deferred annuity

The amount of pension you will get will have been decided when you took out the policy; £x of pension for £y of premiums – for example, paying £1,000 a year for 10 years from the age of 55 to produce a pension of £1,500 a year when you retire at the age of 65.

These are very rarely sold now, but a plan started some years ago may well be of this type.

cash funded plans

The accumulated fund from your invested premiums will be used to buy an annuity at the time when you retire. So the pension you get will depend on the amount you have paid in premiums, the return on the investment of the premiums by the insurance company or other provider, and the annuity rates at the time you retire. For example, if you have been paying in £1,000 a year since the age of 55, you might find the accumulated fund has grown to £20,000 by the time you are 65. If annuity rates at the time are 10%, your pension would be £2,000 a year.

Annuity rates depend on the interest rates available from long-term government stocks. If these are low, the annuity rate will also be low. If at the same time (as happened for instance in the autumn of 1987) the price of shares in the stock market has fallen, your pension may be lower than you expect. You may want then to delay your retirement for a year or two until the situation has recovered.

additional benefits

You can also pay for other benefits within the policy, such as a lump sum death benefit (if you die before retirement) or a dependant's pension. You can also arrange for the pension in payment to increase each year. This will, however, mean that the pension starts off considerably lower than if you were buying a level pension, and it will take a decade or more before the same amount of money is paid out.

paying premiums

With nearly all pension policies, you can pay either regular annual premiums or a one-off single premium. With regular premiums, you are committed to paying a fixed amount to the insurance company every year until retirement date. The terms of a particular policy may allow you to vary the amount of each payment or even to miss one occasionally. This is an important advantage for someone who is self-employed, whose earnings may vary from year to year. Otherwise, if you find yourself unable to continue the premiums, the policy will be made 'paid up'. The insurance company will then levy a charge to cover its administration costs and the commission that has been paid to the broker. Your pension at retirement will then depend on the investment of the remaining money, and will be proportionately reduced.

With a single premium policy, there is no further commitment beyond the payment of the one premium to the insurance company. You can make payments at different times to different companies. The commission payable on a single premium policy is a smaller percentage than on a regular annual premium policy.

If in the years leading up to your retirement, you decide you want to increase your potential pension, you would probably get a better return by paying a single premium for a policy than by starting out on regular premium payments.

premiums and tax

Inland Revenue rules allow only a set percentage (17.5% or 20% or 22.5% or 27.5%, depending on age) of 'net relevant earnings' to be paid each year to a personal pension scheme.

'Net relevant earnings' for tax relief purposes are normally your ordinary PAYE earnings, if you are an employee. If you are self-employed, they are broadly defined by the Inland Revenue as "profits immediately derived by an individual from a trade or profession", minus certain deductions to make them net. These include business losses, agreed capital allowances, and expenses which cannot be set off against other income.

You receive full tax relief on these premiums, at your highest rate of tax. This means that all the premiums you pay in will be taken off your gross earnings, reducing your taxable income in that year.

If one spouse in a marriage is in a pensionable job and the other is not, it may well make sense to pay as much as possible into the non-pensionable partner's personal scheme, in order to build up extra pension. The Inland Revenue will not be concerned whether the money to pay these premiums is in fact coming out of the other person's pocket; all they are worried about is that their own limits are not breached.

Where, for example, a wife works part time in a fairly low paid job and her husband is already reaching the maximum limits on his own scheme (perhaps as a result of paying AVCs), putting further money into a pension for his wife will be a tax efficient method of saving for then both.

'carry forward'

Inland Revenue rules allow you to carry forward any tax relief not used up during the previous six years. If premiums paid in respect of any of these years did not reach the limit allowed by the Inland Revenue, the balance of relief can be carried forward. This means that you can pay more than that year's maximum percentage of your earnings, if you can afford to.

In the years leading up to retirement check whether premiums paid in previous years were less than the maximum allowed for the year in which they were made, and calculate accordingly how much you could carry forward to increase your payment in the coming years.

Anyone who is paying into a personal pension plan should keep a record, year by year, of his/her net relevant earnings. A self-employed person can get this figure from his or her accountant at the end of the year. An employed person can tell from the P60 issued by the employer at the end of the tax year. Against this earnings figure, put the amount of premiums you have paid in the year, the percentage this is of your net relevant earnings for the year, and by how much this was less than the maximum figure allowed for tax relief in that tax year. Then you can take advantage of the carry-forward provisions in any year when you can pay more than that year's maximum for tax relief, and can tell the Inland Revenue how much is to be used from which of the past six years.

'carry back'

It is also possible for a premium paid in any one tax year to be treated for tax purposes as if it had been paid in the previous year, provided you make the necessary 'election' in time. The election has to be made within the year of assessment during which the premium is paid, by writing to your local tax inspector, or by using form 43, available from the tax office.

If you want, and can afford, to pay as much as possible in one year, you can combine the tax advantages of carry-forward and carry-back.

Inland Revenue booklet IR78 *Personal pensions* includes details of how the tax reliefs work.

With all types of approved pension policies, no tax is charged on the fund which accumulates through the investment of the premiums you paid, and the cash sum you take at retirement is tax free. So taking into account also the tax relief on the premiums you are paying, these pension schemes are a very efficient way of saving for your retirement.

the policies

The three main types of policy you can buy are with-profits, unit-linked and deposit administration.

with-profits

With one of these, the insurance company or other provider gives a guarantee of what will be the minimum pension available to you, or the minimum amount of money that will be available to you for buying an annuity at the time you have decided you want to retire. But each year when the company makes a profit on its investments it allocates a part of this profit to its policy holders. This is called a 'bonus' or 'reversionary bonus' and once it is allocated, it cannot be taken away again.

On top of this, at the end of the policy's term the insurance company add a special 'terminal bonus' which gives you a further share in their profits. This, too, is sometimes called by other names – 'final bonus', a 'vesting bonus', a 'maturity bonus' or a 'capital bonus'. This terminal bonus is never guaranteed, and you will not know how much it will be, or whether one will be paid at all, until the moment comes. Often in the recent past the terminal bonus has provided half or more of the fund available at retirement. Insurance companies make great play of their high terminal bonuses, often omitting to point out that this is money that has been held back from earlier bonus payments.

The total sum is used to provide your annuity or pension.

unit-linked

With a 'unit-linked' policy, each premium buys units in a selected fund or several different funds. These funds are managed by the insurance company, unit trust, or other provider. They are invested in different sectors of the investment market. Some funds are very specialist, while others cover a broad range of sectors, so spreading the risk for the investor.

Some unit-linked policies guarantee a minimum sum when you cash the policy. They may say, for instance, that you will get back not less than the total premiums paid. Some guarantee a minimum annuity rate on retirement. But these guarantees tend to be pretty low.

Nearly all unit-linked policies are on a cash funded basis. So that amount of pension you get will depend not only on how the investments have done, but also on annuity rates at the time you want to use the fund to buy a pension.

One problem with a unit-linked pension policy is that at the time when the policy is due to mature, investment conditions may make it a bad time to cash in the units. It is generally considered prudent, therefore, when retirement is just a few years away, to switch the units into a guaranteed fund, and to invest the last two or three years' money in the same way. This will give a guaranteed return, and the fund is certain to grow over the last two or three years before you come to draw a pension. It is important to check in good time whether your policy allows you to switch in that way, and then to remember to exercise your option as retirement approaches. The trick is to time the switch when unit prices are high.

Some insurance companies draw attention to the guaranteed fund when they send out renewal literature to policy holders who are nearing retirement.

deposit administration schemes

These 'policies' operate in much the same way as an investment account at a bank or building society. Your premiums go into an account with the insurance company, and interest is added to it at regular intervals. The interest rate will vary according to the general level of interest rates. Different insurance companies, and other providers, use different methods of allocating and calculating the interest that is added to each account. Often, the interest rate is linked to a quoted index. This might be building societies' current mortgage rates, or the return on fixed interest investments. A few companies guarantee a minimum interest rate.

If you buy one of these policies from an insurance company, it will deduct its charges from the premiums you pay, before investing the rest. Some have an annual management charge, while others make a straight deduction of up to 5% from the initial premium. With schemes run directly by banks and building societies, there will usually be no visible charge, but the interest rate paid will be adjusted to reflect their expenses and profit margins.

All deposit administration schemes are cash funded. A few guarantee that the cash produced by the scheme at the time you retire will not be less than a specified amount.

buying an annuity

Whoever the provider of your pension policy, the annuity bought for you at retirement must be with an insurance company. Normally the provider will shop around for the best annuity on the market at the time. This is called the 'open market option'. All 'appropriate personal pension' schemes must have an open market option with them.

Women will generally receive a lower annuity than men, even at the same age, because their life expectancy is considered to be longer. But under the legislation on 'appropriate personal pensions' the annuities bought with the 'protected rights' fund must be unisex. Even under these, however, a woman – because she retires at 60 – will have a different amount from a man retiring at 65.

when can you get the money?

Under the Inland Revenue rules, the pension from an approved pension scheme must start being paid out before the policy holder reaches 75. If your scheme is an old Section 226 scheme, it cannot start being paid out before age 60, except if you work in certain specified occupations. With the new personal pensions, it can be paid from age 50. In either case, though, the age you specify when you take out the policy will be the age at which you are allowed to start receiving the payments. The only exception is in a case of serious ill-health, when you may be able to draw the benefit earlier – but at a much reduced rate.

One way to give yourself some flexibility on this is to set up a number of policies, each with a different retirement date. You will then be able to draw on each in turn, to increase your income over the first decade or so of retirement. Some pension plans can be taken out as a series of separate policies, each one maturing at a different date so that you can phase your retirement by taking an increased amount of pension as the years go on.

when you come to retire

The amount being offered will be either what you were expecting from the deferred annuity for which you have been paying premiums over the years or, with a cash-funded scheme, what the sum accrued in the fund from your premiums will now buy you as an annuity. You will then have to make the calculations about commuting any part of the money into a cash payment. You need to move fairly quickly once the figures have been given to you, as the quotation will not be held at those rates for very long.

There is no need literally to retire. These contracts are insurance contracts, and there are no conditions on what your circumstances must be when you draw on one, provided you are within the time limits specified. A self-employed person may want to carry on working over the age of 60 or 65. Having a pension in payment means that you can reduce the time you spend working and still retain your standard of living.

retiring younger
If you want to draw a pension before the normal age specified in your policy, because ill-health prevents you from going on working at your normal occupation, you need to provide the insurance company with evidence of your genuine incapacity. Usually a doctor's report will be required, to comply with the Inland Revenue rules for paying out a pension early. The pension you get will be a reduced one, based on actuarial calculations. If the reduction seems to you disproportionately steep, you could try challenging the calculations.

There is no other way in which you can draw on a retirement annuity contract before the age specified in the policy.

retiring later
When you reach the age specified in the policy for the pension to become payable, you will be told how much the pension will

be. If you want to postpone drawing it until a later date, tell them at this stage.

You can postpone the moment for drawing the pension for as long as you like, up to your 75th birthday.

The same outlay will buy a bigger annuity, the later the age at which it is taken. This is because your life expectancy will then be shorter, so that the insurance company will be expecting to pay out for a shorter time.

taking a lump sum

When you come to the point of wanting to draw out your personal pension, you will need to decide how much (if any) of the amount available under the policy should be commuted into a cash payment there and then. This will reduce the amount available to provide a pension through an insurance company.

The Inland Revenue allow only part of the money available to be taken as a lump sum, which is tax free, and the rules differ for the old Section 226 schemes and the new, post July 1988 personal pensions.

For Section 226 schemes, the maximum is three times the pension produced by the sum remaining after commutation. For example, if the policy would produce a pension of £7,000 a year, you could instead take a lump sum of £15,000 and have an annual pension of £5,000. Exactly how much you will get depends on your age, and the annuity rates available at the time when you are commuting the pension. It can be up to 35% of the fund.

In personal pension schemes, the lump sum is lower, but much simpler to work out. It is a straight 25% of whatever fund has accumulated for you at retirement, regardless of your age.

points to take into consideration
It can be advantageous to take a cash sum in place of part of your pension. This is because the whole of the pension from a

personal pension policy is taxed as earned income, but if you use your own cash to buy what is called a 'purchased life annuity', only part of the income from this is taxable. The capital element is tax-free. This applies even if the cash for buying the annuity has come from the lump sum obtained by commuting part of a pension fund.

The proportion of the payment from a purchased life annuity that is considered as the tax-free capital element is based on a statutory formula, linked to mortality tables. It will depend on your age when you take out the annuity. The older you are, the higher the capital element so the less tax on your annuity payments. The insurance company will tell you at the beginning what the capital element is.

You may also feel that you can use the cash payment more profitably by skilful investment, which will more than compensate for the pension foregone.

option to transfer

A cash funded policy taken out since 1978 or so will almost certainly include what is called an 'open market' option. Many of those taken out earlier have also been amended to include a slightly restricted version of the option. This means that a policy holder who has built up a cash fund with one insurance company or other provider, can use it at retirement to buy an annuity with whatever insurance company is offering the best rate at the time.

Having been told what cash sum is available, you can undertake a shopping exercise to find out where this will buy you the best pension, or get a financial adviser to do it for you.

The insurance company which has produced a good return on investments may not necessarily be offering the best rates for a retirement annuity at the date of your retirement.

This option also means that you can put together in one

place all the funds built up from various single premium policies.

Some insurance companies encourage policy-holders to stay with them by offering a bonus of between 1% and 5% on the accrued fund, if it is used to buy an annuity with them. Others penalise policy holders who take up the option to move their money, by making a charge of of 5% of the value of the fund for arranging to do so. This bonus or penalty has to be taken into account when you are looking for a better rate of annuity on the market.

If the policy you are dealing with is an old style Section 226 policy, taking up your 'open market option' means reducing the amount of money you can have as a lump sum to the new personal pension rate (a quarter of the fund). This can make a difference of several hundred pounds or more of lump sum, but on the other hand you could have a larger pension as a result. Find out about both figures and weigh up what is most important to you.

getting a quotation

What you are looking for is a quote for a 'substituted annuity'. The rates for these are slightly different from those for immediate annuities, so that it is important that you specify that this is what you want. The insurance company then knows that the funds for the annuity are coming from an approved pension policy, and that the annuity will therefore be liable to tax on the total payment.

The rates for substituted annuities are quoted regularly in financial magazines such as *Planned Savings* and *Pensions Management*, which should be available in reference libraries or from newsagents. Alternatively, you could telephone a selection of life insurance companies yourself and ask for a quotation. You may, however, prefer to consult a specialist life or pensions broker, who will get you a range of comparable calculations.

The steps you need to take are

1. ask the insurance company you have been paying premiums to how much has accumulated in your fund;
2. ask what pension this would produce if left with that company, how much you would be allowed to take as a lump sum and what this would mean in terms of the pension that was left;
3. check if there would be a charge if you transferred your fund, or a bonus if you did not;
4. get quotations for a substituted annuity contract from a number of other insurance companies;
5. work out what lump sum you could take under the new personal pension rules (a quarter of the fund);
6. if the substituted annuity will be bigger than the pension from the previous scheme (after taking account of any bonus or penalties), you would normally want to take up the option to transfer, unless it is important to you to retain the full value of the Section 226 lump sum.

The law does not allow the money to be paid over to you; the original insurance company will pass the cheque direct to the new one. It then deals with you according to the terms of the new contract.

tax on your pension
The pension that comes from a retirement annuity is liable to tax. The insurance company will normally pay it net of basic rate tax. A higher rate taxpayer will then have to pay the difference by making separate lump sum payments to the Inland Revenue. If you are below the tax threshold (after taking the age allowance into account, if you qualify), ask the insurance company to pay you the gross amount. If you do not do this, you will need to claim tax refunds periodically from the Inland Revenue.

providing for your dependants

Nearly all personal pension policies offer the option to guarantee that payment of the pension will continue for a specified number of years, usually five. If you should die within that time, the payments would continue to be made to your spouse or other nominated dependant for the rest of the guaranteed period. If you take up this option, your own pension will be reduced.

If you live beyond the guaranteed period, nothing will be paid to your spouse or dependant when you die.

If a guarantee does not form part of the initial contract, the insurance company will probably ask you at the time you reach retirement age whether you want a guaranteed period of payment, and to whom payment should be made if you were to die within that period.

Some insurance companies offer a widow's or widower's 'reversionary annuity' – also called a 'joint life and survivor annuity'. This means there is a continuing pension to your widowed spouse. This can be either the same as the amount you will have been getting, or a percentage of your pension. Which option you take will dictate the size of the pension you yourself get.

life insurance
Up until the date you start to draw your pension, you can make provision for your dependants by taking out a life insurance policy which will pay out a tax-free lump sum or a series of lumps sums to your dependants after your death. With life insurance, the premiums are higher the older you are, as the risk is higher.

Under the old arrangements, you were able to buy a Section 226A policy along with the Section 226 retirement annuity policy. You can now buy a policy linked to the new personal pension scheme. In both cases, so long as it is linked to a pension, you can have full tax relief. This is particuarly attractive now that tax relief has been abolished on ordinary life insurance policies taken out since March 1984. However, once you stop paying into the personal pension scheme, you must also stop paying into the life insurance policy.

To get full tax relief, the premiums must in any one year not come to more than 5% of your net relevant earnings. They will count as part of the 17.5% limit on how much you can invest in a personal pension scheme each year.

The policy need not be simply a standard policy offering a fixed lump sum. It can be an increasing term assurance, which means that the later you die, the larger the lump sum, or a decreasing term assurance, which means that the later you die, the smaller the lump sum (and the lower the premiums you have to pay). Or you can take out a term assurance that provides 'family income benefit' in which the equivalent of the lump sum is paid in instalments from the date of your death until the end of the policy term. You can arrange for this to be an escalating benefit so that the amount goes up each year. With some of these policies, the premium stays the same throughout. With others, it increases in line with the increase in the benefit that would be paid. It may be better to choose a policy with which the benefit payable increases from the year after you start the policy, rather than one with which the amount increases only after your death.

Since 1980, it has been possible to arrange for the benefits from this sort of insurance policy to be paid 'under trust'. This means that, on your death, the sum insured can be paid out straightaway to the beneficiary you have nominated, without having to go into your estate. It then does not count for inheritance tax either. All that the trustees have to do on your death is produce a valid death certificate to the insurance company, and payment from the policy can be made without delay. If you have an old Section 226A policy, it may be possible to arrange now for it to be written under trust – check with the insurers.

You do not have to buy the life insurance policy from the same insurance company as the one with which you took out the personal pension. It may be administratively convenient to do so, but the insurance company which offers an attractive pension plan may not be so competitive on life insurance. Some companies do not charge the usual administration fee for issuing a life insurance policy if you already have an approved pension policy with them, so this point also needs weighing up.

When taking out a policy, you need to decide how long you want the term to be. This will probably depend on how near you are to retirement, your age and that of your dependants. Once you are no longer contributing to a personal pension or a Section 226 retirement policy, you are not allowed to carry on with the life insurance policy linked to it.

sources of information

Make sure in good time that you have all the information relevant to your own circumstances, and that you understand all the provisions. The insurance company should be able to help you with any queries you have about the terms of the contract and what pension it should produce. Ask about any choices you may be able to make at this stage to alter the terms of the contract, and the effects of any options.

Detailed information about different policies, insurance companies' performances, current annuity rates, and so on, is published by specialist magazines. Those to look for are *Planned Savings, Money Management, Pensions Management, The Savings Market*. These are expensive publications, but copies should be available in a public reference library. Also, *Which?* publishes reports from time to time on pensions (state and private) and has regular reports on money matters and investment.

The Inland Revenue publish a free pamphlet (IR78) on the tax rules for personal pensions; available from your local tax office.

The **Superannuation Funds Office**, Lynwood Road, Thames Ditton, Surrey KT7 0DP (telephone 01-398 4242), a department of the Inland Revenue, is responsible for seeing that pensions schemes meet the rules for approval under the relevant tax legislation. The SFO can be asked about any statutory restrictions or conditions relating to personal pensions or the old Section 226 schemes. They will not, however, give any sort of advice on individual cases.

You may want general information about personal pension schemes, or about where to go for individual advice. There are various bodies which can supply a list of members operating in a particular area.

The Campaign for Independent Financial Advice, 33 St. John Street, London EC1M 4AA

CAMIFA has an answering service on 01-200 3000 through which they will list for you the names and addresses of a number of independent intermediaries in your area.

British Insurance and Investment Brokers Association, BIIBA House, 14 Bevis Marks, London EC3A 7NT (telephone 01-623 9043)

BIIBA can give you the names of member firms locally and publishes a directory of insurance brokers for the whole country.

Association of British Insurers, Aldermary House, Queen Street, London EC4N 1TT (telephone 01-248 4477)

ABI is the trade association of insurance companies and publishes a series of general leaflets about pensions and life insurance.

The Financial Intermediaries, Managers and Brokers Regulatory Association, Hertsmere House, Marsh Wall, London E14 9RW (telephone 01-538 8860)

FIMBRA is the self-regulating watch-dog body for independent financial advisers. Over 9000 investment brokers are authorised by FIMBRA and must display the FIMBRA member logo on all advertising and business stationery. They are subject to a number of rules of conduct and regular checks by FIMBRA officers. You can check with FIMBRA whether an adviser is properly authorised, or with the Central Register of SIB (**Securities and Investment Board**, 3 Royal Exchange Buildings, London EC3V 3NL, telephone 01-283 2474).

Life Assurance and Unit Trust Regulatory Organisation, Centre Point, 103 New Oxford Street, London WC1A 1QH (telephone 01-379 0444)

LAUTRO is made up of insurance companies, unit trusts and friendly societies, and mainly regulates the marketing of their investments.

PRE-RETIREMENT COURSES

Some employers and companies think that it is their responsibility to prepare their staff for retirement. Some employees are reluctant to attend pre-retirement courses, perhaps because they do not want to think about, or plan for, their own retirement.

A pre-retirement course might cover sessions on the following subjects:

○ pensions (occupational and state) and tax
○ reduced income, wills
○ health: keeping fit, exercise, nutrition
○ leisure, work, voluntary work
○ concessions: travel and other, and how to find out
○ housing, moving, making your house more convenient.

If your firm does not provide a pre-retirement course, the **Pre Retirement Association**, 19 Undine Street, London, SW1 8PP (telephone 01-767 3225) may be able to provide courses or seminars to meet a particular requirement or date, or to give you advice on what courses are available in your area. The Association is mainly concerned with encouraging pre-retirement education. The majority of members are companies, but private individuals can join; generally they join their local, affiliated, organisation.

There are some forty local Pre Retirement Associations (in some localities known as Pre Retirement Council or Retirement Association, or Pre Retirement Committee.) They include GLAP, the **Greater London Association for Pre Retirement**, c/o Babcock Power, 165 Great Dover Street, London SE1 4YB (telephone 01-232 4968) and PRAGMA the **Pre Retirement Associa-**

tion of Greater Manchester, St. Thomas Centre, Ardwick Green North, Manchester M12 6FZ (telephone 061-273 7451) and may be country-wide or concentrate on a single locality. You can find out the address of your nearest Pre Retirement organisation from the PRA headquarters in London.

Choice, the monthly magazine of the Pre Retirement Association, available from newsagents at £1.20, gives advice on a variety of topics, including health, housing and finance. An annual subscription (£16) can be taken out from Choice Publications Ltd, Apex House, Oundle Road, Peterborough PE2 9NP (telephone 0733-555123).

The Open University runs a course called *Planning Retirement* which invites people approaching retirement to examine their own experience and expectations in making realistic decisions for the future. The course consists of a study pack costing £25 and an (optional) assessment pack costing £15, available from the **Open University** Learning Materials Service office, PO 188, Milton Keynes MK7 6DH.

Preparation for retirement is obviously concerned with hard practical matters – health, finance, housing. It also should help to prepare you for more leisure, for the change in family and emotional relationships and how the change in routine will affect you in your new life.

LEARNING TO ENJOY LEISURE

Even someone who has been looking forward to retirement as an opportunity to expand his or her interests and develop a new lifestyle will need a period of adjustment after the many years of regular employment. When suddenly there are no deadlines to be met, no regular journeys to get to work, no need to leave the home at a specific time every day, and the whole day is yours, you may wonder what to do with all this freedom. When free time is unlimited, you may need to exert more self-discipline than you would have imagined, in order to do even the things you most enjoy.

Leisure can be used to do things out of interest rather than for money, doing what you have always wanted to do – including pottering around, gossiping, reading with your feet up and relaxing.

During your working life, if you spent your time in a very sociable environment, it may have been a relief to get away on your own. In retirement, however, you may feel the need for company of like-minded people and therefore decide to join an association, club or group. There are groups and associations for most leisure activities, and being one of a group also imposes some discipline, which is a good thing for someone who no longer has the usual everyday contact with fellow workers.

It may be possible to join an amateur dramatic or an amateur operatic society, not necessarily as the leading tenor or even to take a walk-on part, but helping behind the scenes, to make props, to sew costumes, to be the 'resident handyman , to sell programmes on the night.

Remember that it is more important to enjoy the activity

than to achieve perfection. If you are hesitant about speaking in front of people, take a public speaking course. However, be realistic. Not many people are going to change drastically in late middle age. While inside every shy retiring mouse there may be an extrovert lion trying to get out, if that has not happened by the age of 58, it is unlikely to happen after a public speaking course at 62 or 68. Or if you have 'always wanted to write novels' but never found the time to put pen to paper, it is unlikely that you will turn into a Jane Austen at 61 – but what you write may get published. Or do you enjoy a good read but would like to try something a bit different?

book groups

Reading is, in its essence, a solitary activity, so that even those people who are devotedly fond of books may feel daunted, rather than delighted, at the thought of having all the time in the world for reading. Membership of a book group is a way many people have discovered of giving extra point and interest to their reading, and one which brings with it the pleasure of companionship with people who have similar tastes and interests.

Setting up a book group is very simple: the arrangements can be extremely informal, and all the better for being so. A number of people (four is probably a minimum) agree to get together at regular intervals – say, once a month – to discuss some book which they have previously decided to read. The book is chosen by common consent from suggestions supplied by the members.

The meetings take place in the members' homes, by rotation; the host/hostess offers simple refreshments, such as coffee and biscuits. There is no subscription. No office-holders are required, although one member should be willing to keep a list of members' names and addresses, and a record of books read; but even this 'office' can be rotated. Anybody who has an interested friend should feel welcome to bring him or her along.

Books are expensive, and this can be a difficulty for people on retirement incomes. It is usual for book groups to choose some work that is available in paperback, which means that unless one chooses to read the classics only, the group's reading of modern literature is bound to be at least a year later than first publication. This should not matter; it even gives members an extra incentive to scan book reviews and note likely candidates, to be seized on as soon as they go into paperback.

If the meetings are at monthly intervals, as is usual, this allows time for one or two copies to be read and passed on by several members. Libraries can be useful, and so can second-hand bookshops and charity shops.

what happens depends on you

With regard to the types of books chosen, and the form the discussions take, each group is likely to find its own level before long. The chances are that the founder-members first got together because they enjoyed the same sort of books, anything from Proust to Barbara Cartland, and anyone else who joins in will either fit in or, very soon, drop out. The discussion, too, can be on any level the group finds congenial, from gossip about the fictional characters, to analysis of the author's literary technique.

At the point in the meeting when the words 'shall we make a start?' are uttered, a tongue-tied hush generally descends, so it is just as well that most groups soon develop a 'natural leader' who can be trusted to start the ball rolling (and keep it in motion). But it may be a better idea to appoint at each meeting someone to undertake the task of starting off the discussion at the next meeting.

A book group is not – and should not be – like an academic seminar: much of a group's attraction lies in the social aspect.

There is always a good deal of non-literary chat, at the beginning and end, and other social activities may arise naturally. Visits may be arranged to museums, theatres and concerts; and there can be a Christmas party or a summer outing of some kind. With this encouragement – but even without it – new friendships, which may be continued out of meeting times, naturally follow.

Some of the book groups now in existence started as offshoots of National Women's Register activities, for the benefit of stay-at-home women, and are thus exclusively, or predominantly, female. But there seems no reason why this rule should be followed by the retired, for whom the stimulus of mixed company may be even more important, after years of work in a mixed-gender environment.

leisure for learning

One of the real pleasures of retirement is being able to spend more time on hobbies and interests. Learning a new skill can be immensely satisfying. There are literally hundreds of part time courses available, at all levels, and age is not usually a barrier. Contrary to some people's beliefs, it is never too late to learn.

New activities you may not have thought of, but may want to try include:

brass rubbing, calligraphy, car maintenance, cooking, copper/pewter work, corn-dolly craft, dressmaking, embroidery, jewellery making, lampshade making, leathercraft, macrame, marquetry, painting, pottery, sketching, soft furnishing, weaving, woodwork.

Despite cuts in education budgets, if there is a strong demand for a particular type of class, most authorities will do their best to try to meet it. Classes may include: astronomy, comparative religions, creative writing, genealogy, languages, musical appreciation, philosophy, public speaking, yoga. The cost of classes varies from area to area, but there may be some reduction for retired people.

The **National Extension College**, 18 Brooklands Avenue, Cambridge CB2 2HN offers 10 per cent discount on home-study courses to members of the Pre Retirement Association.

The **University of the Third Age** (U3A) promotes self-help educational activities – run, taught and attended by retired people who are encouraged to contribute their own particular skill, knowledge and experience, and to learn from those of other members. U3A's administration work is largely done by member volunteers. It is open to all retired or unemployed people. There are no upper age limits and no tests for admission. The range of courses and their standards depends on the needs and capacities of specific groups of members, who themselves decide what courses and activities to offer. Individual annual membership in London costs £13, couples £24 and £1 for those on income support and the housebound. But each area has different fees. There are around 100 groups varying in size from 12 to 2000 members. Each group organises and runs its own programme and sets its own fees. For information about local groups, send a stamped self-addressed envelope to the University of the Third Age, Executive Secretary, National Office, c/o BASSAC, 13 Stockwell Road, London SW9 9AU who will advise you on fees and programmes.

The **Worker's Educational Association** (WEA) has over 80 years of experience in providing courses in which all manner of questions are raised and answered. Why is the local landscape as it is? Who first lived in it? What happened next? The WEA offers courses around many interests, some courses are offered in conjunction with the local university. No educational qualifications or formal training is required. You will find like-minded adults who bring different experiences of life to the group and who are enjoying the guidance around the subject that a skilled tutor can give.

Your first meeting can be a 'free sample' – you attend (where vacancies exist) without commitment. Classes usually meet weekly for up to 20 weeks in the spring and autumn terms. The tutor will suggest books for reading as inclination and time allows, but homework is not usually expected.

In some areas, courses are also offered in the summer term. These are probably field study courses when you go out to look at your local landscapes, architecture, industrial heritage, or natural world and find out what an expert sees there. In addition, there may be excursions arranged to interesting places and events, or other activities which are both informative and sociable.

Your local library carries the brochure of courses, especially around September time; or they can give you the name of the local branch secretary.

The WEA is a national voluntary movement with a skeleton of professional staff. The tutors are almost all part-time. So beginning as a student, you could join the branch committee, and then serve at county, district or even national level. Or if you have the knowledge, you could offer a subject to the local branch committee.

If there is no branch near you, write to the head office of the WEA: if all else fails, they may help you start a branch. The address is Worker's Educational Association, 9 Upper Berkeley Street, London W1H 8BY (telephone 01-402 5608).

short courses

A continuous course with regular meetings requires the place where you meet to be fairly close, but for a one-day course you can go further afield. Day schools (as they are usually called) mostly take place on a saturday, and offer the opportunity to study some aspect of your subject more intensively, and to meet other enthusiasts. They may be offered by the local WEA, or the local university, or by some other organisation. Your library should have the brochures, or ring the local university and ask for their 'extra-mural department' (or it may have a name like 'centre for continuing education'). They will be delighted to send you a copy of their programme. London University also offers day schools on a range of subjects in central London.

Some universities offer weekend courses occasionally; Oxford and Cambridge extra-mural departments have their own excellent accommodation, and offer residential weekends throughout the year. There are also many residential colleges and other organisations throughout the country who offer weekend courses on a vast range of subjects. Prices are from around £40-£45 for one night or £60-£65 for two nights (for a shared bedroom), full board and all the tuition.

The most comprehensive catalogue, listing in outline some 2000 courses on nearly 100 subjects is produced twice yearly, mid-winter and mid-summer by the **National Institute of Adult Continuing Education**, and costs about £1.20. You need then to ask the organisation of your choice for further details. These are free.

If you want to enjoy a whole week doing what you like or take a study tour abroad, the WEA, some universities and other organisations offer study tours on (for example) the sculpture of classical Greece, the architecture of Sicily, or the fascinations of the Far East. Or the **Field Studies Council** (if no-one else) will take you to the volcanoes of Italy or the jungle of Malaysia – and bring you back.

There is no need to go abroad: there is much of interest at home. Oxford University at Rewley House, near the centre of the city, and London University at a country mansion at Westonbirt, Gloucester organise summer schools covering about a dozen subjects a week for 3 weeks in July-August. You should be prepared to do some reading beforehand, to want to express your views in a written essay and to discuss them with your tutor.

The Summer Academy organised by the School of Continuing Education at the University of Kent is run on different lines. Their holidays covering about 67 courses are arranged in conjunction with 8 other universities throughout the country, and are spread from July to September. Written work is not expected.

Other universities and organisations also offer holidays where you can develop your interest. Play music at Benslow, paint at Weobley, study and walk in the countryside with the Field Studies Council, hammer away at the geology of Cumbria. All these and many others are listed in the NIACE booklet.

You are not expected to be an expert to share in these holidays, and they will not make you into one. All that is needed is a keen interest and a readiness to share the enthusiasm of the tutors and your fellow-students for the subject. And there is time to relax and see the sights and enjoy the social life. But it can be the most stimulating holiday you have ever had and you may come away with friends for life.

If you are feeling energetic, are under 71, and conservation is your thing, you can have a 'Natural Break' organised by the **British Trust for Conservation Volunteers**. You can tackle coppicing, sand dunes, drystone walling, path work and other real conservation work. You make a donation to the Trust to cover accommodation and food. As a holiday it is cheap but you are kept busy and the accommodation can be quite basic.

some useful addresses

British Trust for
Conservation Volunteers
36 St Mary's Street
Wallingford
Oxon OX10 0EU

National Institute of
Adult Continuing Education
19B De Montfort Street
Leicester LE1 7GE
telephone: 0533 551451

University of Cambridge
Board of Extra Mural Studies
Madingley Hall
Madingley
Cambridge CB3 8AQ
telephone: 0954 210636

University of London
Centre for Extra-Mural Studies
26 Russell Square
London WC1B 5DQ
telephone: 01-636 9720
            (24 hour answerphone)
            01-636 8000
            (main switchboard)

University of Oxford
Department of External Studies
Rewley House
1 Wellington Square
Oxford OX1 2JA
telephone: 0865 270360

The Field Studies Council
Preston Montford
Montford Bridge
Shrewsbury SY4 1HW
telephone: 0743 850614

Worker's Educational Association
9 Upper Berkeley Street
London W1H 8BY
telephone: 01-402 5608

Summer Academy
School of Continuing Education
The University
Canterbury
Kent CT2 7NX
telephone: 0227 470402
            (24 hour answerphone)

concessions

Once you reach state retirement age (65 or 60) you will qualify
for a number of concessions and benefits. For some, you need
proof of age, and perhaps proof that you are a resident of the
area; for others, you have to be able to produce your pension
book. Someone having the pension paid directly into the bank,
should ask the local social security office for form BR 464, so that
a card giving proof of retirement age can be sent from the
Department of Social Security; this card can be used instead of
a pension book to obtain concessions.

Some theatres offer reductions for matinees or some mid-
week evening performances, usually one ticket per person – so
if you go with someone below retirement age, you may sit
side-by-side for different prices.

Local authority concessions vary from area to area, but might include reduced entrance to swimming baths at off-peak times of day; waived fines on overdue library books; museums, stately homes, art galleries and exhibitions that normally charge an entrance fee may waive or reduce it. Some clubs and associations offer membership at a reduced fee or allow non-members over retirement age to buy tickets (such as the National Film Theatre in London). Many ordinary cinemas offer seats at half-price for their afternoon performances. The admission fee for some sports events may be reduced.

Even private businesses, such as dry cleaners and hair-dressers, may offer reductions.

All this varies from place to place, so you will have to keep your eyes open for notices and, if in doubt, ask if there is an OAP reduction.

NHS concessions

When you reach the official state retirement age, prescriptions are free. Just tick the box on the back of the prescription form and fill in the details in the space provided.

bus and coach

Most local bus companies, both those run by the local authority and privately run ones, let senior citizens travel either free or at reduced rates. There may be restrictions, such as no conces-sionary travel during certain hours.

Find out what the situation is in your area, from the local bus company; a bus conductor may be a good first contact. National Express reduce their inter-city coach fares by one-third for senior citizens.

trains

The British Rail senior citizen railcard is available to everyone over 60 and costs £15 for one year. The card entitles you to various reductions in fares. At present these are

o one-third discount on off-peak monthly returns ('saver tickets')
o one-third discount on standard single tickets
o one-third discount on standard return tickets
o half price cheap day-returns (off-peak day-returns)
o half price standard day-returns.

You can take four children aged under 16 with you, for a set price per head each. There is also a discount on ferries to the Isle of Wight and the Channel Islands. From time to time some shipping companies offer reduced prices to senior citizens or railcard holders. For travel on inter-city sleeper services you have to pay the full sleeper supplement but only the discounted fare.

At present, a senior citizen railcard also entitles you to reduced travel on the London underground.

There are certain restrictions about trains on which the concessionary fares do not apply. British Rail have leaflets which give up-to-date information.

foreign rail travel
Many of the European railway companies offer reductions to their own senior citizens; most extend these to foreign travellers.

The British Rail senior citizen railcard entitles you to buy, for £5, a Rail Europ senior citizen railcard which gives savings on the cost of travel from the UK to 18 continental countries and on journeys within those countries, namely

o 50 per cent reduction on railways in Belgium, Eire, Finland, France, Greece, Holland, Luxembourg, Portugal, Spain, and most Swiss railways
o 30 per cent in Austria, Denmark, Hungary, Italy, Norway, Sweden, West Germany, Yugoslavia

○ 30 per cent on sea crossings by Sealink, Hoverspeed hover-craft, P&O services between Dover and Ostend or between Portsmouth and Le Havre, when the crossing is part of a rail/sea through journey to points in Europe.

Reductions do not apply to sleeping accommodation, to jet foil supplements, to the supplement payable on some continental services or to travel by Motorail.

The main restriction on the use of a Rail Europ card is on travel which starts in one of the foreign countries during parts of the weekend. But if you start your journey in this country and travel through to your destination without any stopover, the fares reductions do apply even for weekend travel.

holidays

Some tour operators specialise in holidays for older people, which usually means over 55 years of age. The Greater London Association for Pre Retirement has compiled an information booklet *Holidays* (£1.50) which gives details; your local Pre Retirement Association may produce a similar information leaflet.

Most of these holidays are for out-of-season periods.

Travel Companions, 89 Hillfield Court, Belsize Avenue, London NW3 4BE (telephone 01-431 1984) provides a nationwide personal service for people up to the age of 75 who would like to share holidays. You fill in a questionnaire and they choose a compatible person whom you meet before you decide to holiday together. The fee is £35 for three introductions in a year (extended if none of these results in a holiday).

CHIPS (**Cultural Holidays for independent People**), Hillside, Milford, Surrey GU8 5IJ (telephone 04868 25265), arranges three to four-day holidays in Bath, Cambridge, Eastbourne, Oxford, Richmond, York.

Saga Singles Holidays (PO Box 64, Folkestone, Kent CT20 1AZ) are designed for people who do not wish to pay single room supplements.

Solitaire (PO Box 2, Hockley, Essex SS5 4QR) is an organisation which tries to help retired single women in their fight against loneliness by keeping a pen friends and holiday register, and to enable those who live reasonably near to each other to meet and make contact. Membership is free (but send two stamped self-addressed envelopes) and is open only to spinsters and very isolated widows.

exercise and sport

There will be more time for exercise and sports after retirement. If you have been in the habit of taking regular exercise, carry on, or if your work involved a lot of moving about and physical activity, continue with some exercise and using your muscles. If you have not done anything physically active for many years and never thought of doing so, do so now. There is no need to feel that you are too old, or too flabby, or likely to make a fool of yourself. However, do not suddenly take up a new form of strenuous exercise.

Walk, cycle, swim as much as possible, and keep going with any sport you have been doing. If you want to take up a suitable new one, the choice includes badminton, bowls, golf, table tennis. Classes in dancing (country and ballroom), and keep-fit classes are held at adult education centres, and other places, and once you have learned the movements, you can carry on by yourself.

When you are retired, you will be in a position to use sports facilities during the less crowded hours – such as public tennis courts and the swimming pool – at times when you used to be at work. Most public swimming baths charge less to retired people, and some private ones offer concessions to people who use the pool at off-peak times.

Swimming is not only very healthy, at any age, but has the advantage that you do not have to rely on finding a partner or a team. On the other hand, there is an advantage in taking up, or continuing, a sport that allows (or even forces) you to meet others. The **Ramblers' Association** (which promotes rambling, protects rights of way, and campaigns for access to open country) charges a reduced membership fee to retired people. For details, contact The Ramblers 1/5 Wandsworth Road, London SW8 2XX (telephone 01-582 6878).

A good contact is your local sports centre or the recreation department of the local authority. The regional office of the **Sports Council** (headquarters at 16 Upper Woburn Place, London WC1H 0QP, telephone 01-388 1277) will also be able to help with suggestions and local addresses.

The Sports Council has a '50+' leaflet with suggestions for out-and-about activities (such as hiking, rambling, orienteering, bird watching); for 'sports centre activities', including their likely costs and the equipment needed; on 'lending a hand', with suggestions for participating in the activities of a local sports club. This leaflet should be available at your local library.

exercise

Exercise is a vital part of keeping fit and healthy at any age. Regular exercise will lift your mood and improve concentration and generally make you feel better. If you are tired and lacking in energy, it will give you more energy and vitality. You will sleep better and be more relaxed. Your whole body, including your muscles and joints, your bones and major organs will work more efficiently. Your heart will work more effectively, and risk of diseases such as atherosclerosis ('hardening of the arteries') will be reduced.

Exercise is best if it is a regular part of your normal life. So consider using stairs rather than the lift or escalator, walking or cycling instead of taking the car, and including in your leasure time a sport or exercise programme which is a combination of exercise for building stamina and exercise for increasing suppleness. Exercise for building stamina such as swimming, cycling, jogging (on grass, and wearing the proper shoes) should be done about three times a week and leave you feeling a bit sweaty and breathing more heavily. Exercise to increase suppleness includes yoga, a gentle, stretching exercise programme, tai chi, and some forms of dance.

If you are not used to sports, start with only short periods of exercise and gradually and regularly increase the time and vigour. Before embarking on exercise, if it is new to your lifestyle, consider your general fitness level. You should not exercise if you have had a mild illness such as a cold until you are fully recovered. If you have a more serious illness, or have been in hospital or are recovering from influenza or a bad cold, or suffer from hypertension (high blood pressure), arthritis, or indeed have any doubts about the wisdom of regularly exercising, you should seek medical advice about what exercise is safe for you to do. While exercising, never ignore fatigue; take a rest when you are tired. Avoid exercising to the point of severe breathlessness, pain or distress. Stop immediately if you experience chest or leg pains or dizziness or break out in a cold sweat. Rough games such as football are not recommended as you get older. You are more vulnerable to injury which would take longer to heal.

Above all, choose a form of exercise that you enjoy. Start gently, but do it regularly and build it up as you become more fit. The older you are, the more slowly you should go. It is better to do 10–20 minutes daily, rather than 2 hours once a week.

If you plan to do more strenuous exercise, always do a warm up programme beforehand. Without proper warming up, you are at risk of injury. Try to do an exercise programme in a smooth, unhurried fashion. It should not be painful nor feel like an endurance test.

Some people forget to breathe when concentrating on a movement so, when exercising, check your breathing from time to time. Try to let your movements and your breathing flow rhythmically and smoothly together. If you experience any mild discomfort (not pain), slow down, take a few breaths, wait to see if the discomfort has eased. If it has, then continue slowly. If not, stop and move on to another exercise. Never speed up or push on in these circumstances.

As you exercise, try to concentrate on what you are doing so that your body awareness increases. If you notice your attention wandering, then gently bring it back to what you are doing. When you have completed your exercise programme, take time to cool down and to relax.

basic exercise programme

The following is a programme of exercises which could be attempted by people in the middle or third age of life, who are new to exercise and not particularly fit. Later the programme could be used as a warm up to more vigorous exercise.

basic standing and breathing

Start by standing with your feet about shoulder width apart, parallel and straight with your toes pointing straight ahead. Let the weight be slightly forward on the balls of your feet, but keeping your heels on the floor. Let your knees be slightly bent. Your thighs and pelvic area should be loose. Let your buttocks be loose. Let your back be straight, but with loose shoulders. Your shoulders should be down and slightly back without them being held stiffly. Let your arms hang loosely by your side. Your head should be in line with your spine and held up straight, as if you had a string through the top of your head holding you up, but let your chin be tucked in. Take a few deep breaths – breathing gently and smoothly, keeping your shoulders down and not forcing the breath. Breathe all the way down to your abdomen. Feel your feet firmly on the ground and enjoy this sensation. Slowly bend and straighten your knees gently 6 times. Then bend them again and maintain the position for about half a minute, focusing your attention on your breathing and bodily sensations. When you feel ready to continue, gradually straighten up. Give your arms and legs a shake. You may be aware of your legs being warm, tingling, a bit shaky.

Continue with the following to loosen you up and get the blood flowing. Stand once more in the basic standing and breathing position. Start by shaking one hand loosely from the wrist. Imagine that you have something sticky stuck to your fingers, which you are trying to shake off. Let your fingers be loose and heavy. Circle your hand around your wrist. Continue for a minute.

○ Give your lower arm a shake. Let it be heavy and loose. Imagine your muscles loosening and lengthening, and any tension flowing out of your body through the fingers.
○ Give your whole arm a shake. Feel it become heavy.
○ Let your arm rest by your side. Notice any differences between the arm you have been moving and the other one. It may feel lighter or heavier, cooler or warmer, tingling. Now repeat the shaking of the wrist, lower arm and whole arm with the other arm.
○ Make sure that you check your breathing from time to time.

Now concentrate on your legs. You will be standing for a short time balancing on one leg and so you may need to position yourself near a wall or a firm chair to help you in balancing.

○ Begin by moving your weight on to one leg, then gently lift the foot of the other leg. Move your foot up and down, circle it around your ankle. Give it a shake.
○ Shake your lower leg. Let it be loose and heavy.
○ Give your whole leg a shake. And then gently put your foot down on the ground. Feel the difference between the one leg and the other.
○ Repeat with the other leg.
○ Now shrug your shoulders. Move them around – backwards, forwards, up, down, one at a time, two together – loosening them up.
○ Now give your hips a wiggle – let your bottom wobble.
○ Come back to the basic standing and breathing position. Take a few breaths.

How are you feeling? If you are not tired, continue with the next part of the basic exercise programme.

gentle stretching
The following sequence of exercises is designed to stretch and tone the main parts of the body.

Stand in the basic standing and breathing position. Take a few breaths and give yourself time to focus your attention again.

Now consider your eyes. Keep them open and let them look to the right . . . then left . . . up . . . down . . . on to a more distant object and then to one closer. Keep breathing and repeat twice more.

Now consider your mouth and jaw. Open your mouth wide. Move your jaw slowly from side to side, and then slowly move it around more generally.

Check you head now. Make sure that it is straight – in line with your spine and not tilted to either side. Slowly bring your head forward, bringing your chin to rest on your chest. Feel the gentle stretch – breathe and slowly bring it up again. Repeat twice more.

Keeping your eyes open and body facing forward, turn your head slowly to the right. Focus your eyes on a point. Breathe and slowly bring your head back to the mid-point. Repeat twice more on the right. You may find that you can go a little further each time and can judge this by noticing the point that you focus on each time. Never force the movement and always move slowly. Repeat the exercise, but this time turning to the left. Now keeping your eyes forward, tilt your head to the right side as if to touch your shoulder with it. Slowly bring it up. Repeat twice more. Let the weight of the head do the movement, so that there is less effort involved. Now repeat on the left side.

Slowly bring your shoulders up to your ears. And then slowly drop them. Notice your breathing. Repeat twice more.

Now slowly lift up both arms out to the side, and then gradually up above your head. Let them stretch up. Let your fingers stretch up. Keep your feet flat on the ground. Then gradually lower your arms down to your side, keeping the speed consistent, smooth and regular. Repeat twice more and breathe.

Wiggle your fingers around. Imagine that you are playing the piano and move each finger and your thumbs in turn. Stretch your fingers so that there is a wide space between each finger. Bring your hand into a fist and then stretch your fingers out again fanning your fingers wide apart. Repeat 5 or 6 times.

Now move your hand up and down, to the left and right moving around the wrist. Repeat 3 or 4 times.

Keeping your trunk facing forward, stretch one arm down the side of the leg on the same side. Then slowly bring your trunk and arm back to the starting position. Repeat twice more. Then repeat the exercise on the opposite side.

Be very careful with the next two exercises if you have any back problems and leave them out if in doubt.

Stand in the basic standing and breathing position, but with a slightly wider base for your feet. Make both hands into fists and place behind you in the lower back on each side of the spine. Your elbows will be bent. Keeping your feet flat on the ground, gently arch your back. Support your back with your fists and gradually bring your elbows closer together. Let yourself breathe and maintain the position for about half a minute. Then gradually come back to the basic standing and breathing position. You may feel slight trembling in your body.

Now bring your feet slightly closer together and let yourself drop forward from the waist. Let your arms hang loosely, and your neck hang loosely down, pulled down by the weight of your head. Keep your eyes open, continue to breathe. Gradually straighten your knees a little and feel the stretch on the back of your legs. Hold the position for half to one minute. Then slowly begin to unwind from the base of the spine back into the standing position. Take time to be aware of how you are feeling.

Remain in the basic standing and breathing position. Put your hands on your hips. Allow your pelvis to tip backwards and forwards slowly and gently. Keep breathing as you concentrate on this movement. Repeat the forward and backward movement 4 or 5 times. Make sure that it is only your pelvis moving (and not your whole trunk or legs). Notice the stretch on your abdominal muscles and those in your lower back.

You may find it easier to do the next 2 exercises using a chair to help you to balance. Keeping one foot on the ground, lift your other leg with the knee bent as high as you comfortably can, while keeping your back straight. Feel the stretch. Gently lower that leg and lift the other leg in the same way. Repeat 4 or 5 times.

You have now gradually worked through exercising most of the body.

And now let yourself lie down comfortably on your back, with your arms and legs uncrossed. Let yourself relax and take a few breaths, breathing all the way down to your abdomen and all the way out from your abdomen. Let yourself relax and experience the different bodily sensations that the exercises have stimulated.

When you feel ready to sit up, first turn on to your side and rest for a while in that position; then get up from there. Give yourself plenty of time. Don't rush.

sitting exercise programme

This programme is suitable for people who have been ill, are frail or more elderly. Sit in a chair which has a firm seat and back. Make sure it is comfortable: a dining room chair, which is stable, would be suitable.

basic sitting and breathing

Sit so that your feet are flat on the ground about shoulder width apart, parallel and straight with your toes pointing forward. Your hips, knees and ankles should make right angles and your knees should be in line with your ankles. Your back should be straight, but comfortable with your shoulders loosely held down and slightly back. Let your arms hang down loosely by your side, or let your arms and hands be relaxed with your hands resting gently on your thighs. Your head should be in line with your spine and held up straight as if you had a string through the top of your head holding it up. Let your chin be tucked in. Focus your eyes softly in front of you. Take a few deep breaths – breathing gently and smoothly, keeping your shoulders down and not forcing the breath. Breathe all the way down to the abdomen and all the way out from your abdomen. Feel your feet firmly on the ground and enjoy this sensation. Focus your attention on your breathing and bodily sensations. When you feel calm, with your concentration focused on yourself, you may feel ready to continue.

Continue with the exercises to loosen you up and get the blood flowing described on the previous pages, but from a sitting rather than a standing position.

Now concentrate on your legs. Lift one foot and give it a gentle shake. Move it up and down and circle it from the ankle. Then circle it in the opposite direction. Now shake your lower leg. Let it be loose and heavy. Now give your whole leg a shake. And then gently put your foot down on the ground. Feel the difference between the two legs. Now repeat with the other leg.

Now shrug your shoulders. Move them around – backwards, forwards, up, down, one at a time, two together – loosening them up. Now come back to the basic sitting and breathing position. Take a few breaths and notice how you are feeling.

If you feel comfortable, continue. Do the full range of gentle stretching exercises while you sit in the basic sitting and breathing position.

Now you have exercised down through the body. Let yourself sit in the basic sitting and breathing position once more. Let your eyes close and take a few deep breaths, breathing deeply and gently and slowly. Let yourself relax and enjoy the bodily sensations that the exercises have stimulated. When you feel ready, slowly open your eyes. Gradually prepare to get up and carry on with your day. Don't rush: take your time.

YOUR HEALTH

Too many people attribute unpleasant symptoms to age when, in fact, they may have an illness which can be diagnosed and treated. If you feel unwell or notice that you now need to do things in a markedly different way, or avoid doing things, do not dismiss such symptoms as mere signs of approaching age.

Go and see your doctor about any symptoms that worry you, including

○ pain in the chest (sudden or severe or persistent)
○ continuous pain in the abdomen
○ blood from any part of the body – in urine, in stools (making them look black) in sputum, in vomit
○ localised weakness of an arm or leg
○ breathlessness
○ loss of weight
○ hoarseness that persists
○ a lump in the breast, in the groin, in the neck – anywhere in the body
○ fainting
○ the sudden appearance of a mole or change in an existing one or an uneven skin discoloration
○ persistent irritation of the skin, persistent itching, an ulcer
○ unnatural tiredness
○ frequent need to urinate
○ marked change in bowel habits
○ any persistent pain.

The doctor may be able to recognise a potentially serious disease – diabetes, high blood pressure, heart trouble, cancer – in its early stage, and carry out treatment at a time when it can be effective. He can send you for specialist examination if necessary. Many diseases come on insidiously and can be dealt with, or avoided, if action is taken in time.

And if there is nothing seriously the matter, the doctor can reassure you and advise you on what you should do to keep yourself in good health. You should never feel guilty about seeming to waste the doctor's time. There is no reason why you should think that you must put up with pain or discomfort, just because you are getting older. Middle age – or old age – is not an illness.

The Open University sells two packs called *Look after yourself* and *Health and retirement*, intended for group discussion. They are sold in sets at £36 for six. Single-person packs are also available for £8 each. For further information contact the Learning Materials Service Office, **The Open University**, PO Box 188, Milton Keynes MK7 6DH.

taking care of your back

When you are standing or walking, be aware of your posture. Much back trouble can be prevented if the back and abdominal muscles are kept strong and in good tone and if you avoid stress on the spine, particularly in the region of the lower back. Be careful how you lift and carry heavy things.

It is best, particularly if there has been backache or sciatica in the past, to bend at the knees and, keeping the spine straight, lift the object by straightening the knees, not bending the spine at all. Also, easy chairs that are too easy and slouchy car seats should be avoided. If the small of the back is not adequately supported, a small cushion here helps. The Consumer Publication *Understanding back trouble* includes advice on all this and more.

Make sure that your bed is comfortable. If you feel stiff when you wake in the morning, it may be for no other reason than that the bed is unsuitable. For good support, and a comfortable night's rest, the mattress should be firm and should not give by more than about two inches at any part. If your mattress is beginning to sag, buy a new one. Mattresses are expensive and it may therefore be a good idea to buy one before retirement, when you still have more money. Make sure that the one you buy conforms to the Furniture and Furnishings (Fire/Safety) Regulations 1988.

Good mattresses are best on a firm solid base. Although some people think that a so-called orthopaedic mattress would be a good investment for their retirement, there is no evidence that such a mattress would do more for you than any other firm mattress on a good base.

If you have persistent backache, or pain or stiffness in the joints, this may be due to arthritis. Consult your doctor.

arthritis and osteoporosis

There are many different types of arthritis: the most likely one to make its presence felt in a 60 year old is osteoarthritis, largely a degenerative condition affecting the cartilages in knees, hips, big toe joints, finger joints and the spine, particularly in the neck and lower lumbar regions. Inflammation may occur after an injury and fluid (noticeable as a swelling) may appear in the knees, for instance, after twists, strains or other injuries.

It is, however, important to keep supple and mobile, so try to move each and every joint through its full range of movements several times a day. It used to be said that growing old is all too often growing fat; growing stiff is also a danger in this age group. If, on exercise, discomfort is felt in joints, people tend to do less and more limited exercising – which in turn leads to increased stiffness and diminished mobility and weight gain.

If there has been an inflammatory type of arthritis (such as rheumatoid arthritis) previously, there is a great tendency for the affected joints to stiffen and develop contractures (that is, permanent shortening of a muscle or of fibrous tissue). Control of pain and swelling by appropriate drugs may be necessary to maintain mobility. Any new symptoms arising in bones and joints in the sixties should be reported to one's doctor and if necessary investigated further, particularly if there is weight loss and a deterioration in general health or appearance of symptoms in other parts of the body (gastro-intestinal, respiratory or genito-urinary).

Diminished activity tends to lead to osteoporosis (thinning of the bones) in which the long bones become weaker in texture and more liable to fracture and the vertebral bodies to crush and become brittle and wedge-shaped, leading to round shoulders and loss of height. Women past the menopause are more prone to osteoporosis because oestrogen deficiency reduces the body's ability to retain calcium. Hormone replacement therapy can help considerably. The December 1988 edition of *Which? Way to Health* includes an article on HRT.

Research (funded by the charity **Research Into Ageing**) is currently being conducted showing that, for women suffering from osteoporosis, exercises which put a load on the skeleton will strengthen bones and lessen the chance of fracture.

Regular exercise is essential for anyone approaching retirement: where our ancestors walked, rode on horses or bicycles, we tend to step into our car and sit in it in a cramped position, allowing muscles to weaken and joints to stiffen.

There is now a new method of X-ray scanning which can help diagnose bone loss at an early stage, before bones start to fracture. It is a quick technique but at present there are very few screening centres. **The National Osteoporosis Society**, Barton Meade House, PO Box 10, Radstock, Bath BA3 3XB (telephone 0761 32472) publishes information, including a booklet *What Every Woman Needs To Know About Osteoporosis* free to members.

more about exercise

There is growing realisation, supported by research, that a reasonable amount of exercise keeps the older body in trim. No one under at least 75 need be labelled old and, even after that age, increasing frailty can be postponed by exercise. Remember that quite a small loss of muscle power will mean crossing the threshold of dependence. The muscles which enable us to sit and rise from a chair (or loo) unaided must be maintained. Regular walks will help; if walks are impossible, exercising at home becomes essential.

Falls by people aged 65 and over account for 52% of deaths from domiciliary accidents. Muscle weakening and wasting are important contributory factors. To prevent a stumble becoming a fall depends not only on postural control but on the development of power output in lower limb and trunk muscles. The strength of elderly muscles can be increased by appropriate physical training. A recent study of 58 men and 67 women mostly aged 65 to 75 demonstrated statistical associations between calf muscle strength and chosen walking speed and, in men, the number of steps taken per day. This suggests that a high level of customary activity may help protect against some of the age-associated loss of muscle mass and performance.

Sitting quietly, unless one has to, is likely to increase the possibility of greater immobility with all its attendant risks.

sleeping and eating

People differ in the amount of sleep they need. By and large, an adult's pattern of sleep is retained until the onset of old age. But there can be temporary upsets due to worry, pain or other physical disturbances.

Sleep is a habit which, if it is broken for whatever reason, can sometimes be difficult to re-establish. Because one of the causes of insomnia is worry and stress, the worry (justified or not) about retirement and change of lifestyle associated with it, may make a previously sound sleeper develop less regular sleeping habits.

Insomnia is the persistent inability, real or imagined, to sleep. Anyone waking up very early feeling fresh and well has probably had enough sleep and is not suffering from real insomnia. However, people who repeatedly wake in the early hours and feel tired and depressed should consider getting help from their doctor.

People who take little exercise, or sit and doze in an armchair all the evening, should not expect to fall asleep the minute they go to bed and then to sleep all night. It might be a good idea to take a brisk walk before going to bed, as part of a regular bedtime routine. Some people find that a hot milky drink last thing at night will help them sleep, but they should not be misled into believing that special branded bedtime drinks have some particular sleep-giving quality; these have no advantage over any other non-stimulant hot drink. It is the routine that matters and can help people who have difficulty in falling asleep.

At any age, people feel better, look better and on the whole are generally healthier if they are not overweight and eat a sensible balanced diet, get adequate sleep and exercise.

A well-balanced mixed diet contains protein (meat, eggs, fish) carbohydrates (bread, potatoes, rice), fats (margarine, milk, cheese), vitamins and minerals in fresh fruit and vegetables.

Wholemeal bread, coarse green vegetables, salads, unpeeled fruit and bran all help to provide fibre in the diet. Vitamin D, which is needed along with calcium to maintain healthy bones, is found in eggs, liver, salt-water fish and is formed in the skin following exposure to sunlight.

The body requires at least three pints of liquid a day so that the kidneys can function effectively. There is no harm in beer or wine, in moderation, but too much alcohol can lead to health problems, quite apart from the other costs.

If you were used to eating lunch at your office or works canteen, make sure that after retirement you will continue having at least one proper meal each day when you have to provide it yourself. Try not to make up for missed meals by getting through packets of biscuits. Being at home all day you may be tempted to eat more: make sure that you keep an eye on your weight, following your retirement.

If you eat more than your energy expenditure requires, you get fat. Carrying too much weight makes people more liable to develop diabetes and diseases of the heart, and may aggravate arthritis.

diabetes in older people

In older age groups, diabetes is different from that seen in young people who can become suddenly very ill and require insulin injections to stay alive.

Some 85% of diabetes occurs in the older age groups. It usually develops slowly over some months, with the symptoms of thirst (sometimes extreme) and passing extra urine. Extreme tiredness then develops. If these symptoms are prominent, and especially if they have developed rather rapidly, it is advisable to see a doctor as soon as possible.

Some of the long-term problems which may be caused by diabetes or by other conditions may bring the person to a doctor, anyway – for example visual problems (retina/cataracts), foot ulcers and leg pains either due to nerve damage or blood vessel disease and also trouble with angina and heart disease. So, obviously, if you are suffering from any of these it is wise to check that diabetes is not part of the problem. The doctor can do this by a simple blood test.

However, many people have this form of diabetes (non-insulin dependent diabetes or type 2 diabetes) without ever knowing, and the diagnosis comes to light during other medical examinations.

Treatment with insulin is rarely necessary in older people with diabetes. Control of carbohydrate foods (sweet foods, soft bread, cake and biscuits, alcohol) is the central part of treatment. The modern approach to diabetic dieting – which will help with weight as well – allows quite a good intake of fibre foods such as vegetables, fruit, wholemeal bread and so on, with some slight reduction in the amount of fat eaten. Such treatment tends to lead to some weight loss and lowering of the blood sugar. But if the sugar does not come down satisfactorily, there are some drugs available to help with this.

Essentially, diabetes at this age is not too difficult to keep under control although it does require a degree of discipline, particularly with regard to diet.

regular check-ups: teeth, eyes, and ears

If you suspect that your hearing is not as sharp as it once was, go to your general practitioner for a check-up. You should not accept the doctor telling you that people must expect hearing problems as they get older. If the GP cannot find a cause for the loss of hearing (such as wax in the ear which he can syringe), he should refer you to the ENT (ear, nose and throat) clinic at the local hospital. Following a hearing test, you may be told that a hearing aid may help you. Hearing aids are available on the NHS or privately. The report in *Which?* January 1988 (which refers to an extended report in *Self Health* December 1987) warns against misleading advertisements and hard-sell visits from sales reps.

The **Royal National Institute for the Deaf**, 105 Gower Street, London WC1E 6AH (telephone 01-387 8033) publishes quarterly a magazine *Sound Barrier* and a range of other books and leaflets. The RNID offers a free hearing advisory service (advice, hearing tests, a comprehensive range of aids for users to evaluate).

teeth

Neglect in middle age can quite unnecessarily lead to losing your teeth. Make a dental appointment at least once a year even if your mouth seems healthy, but particularly if you show signs of bleeding, bad breath or loose teeth. You should go to a dentist who is prepared to take trouble with your gums and give your teeth regular scaling.

If you have dentures, get them checked every three years, because the shape of the mouth changes and dentures must be adjusted. Any lumps on the gums or persistent soreness should be investigated by the dentist.

eyes

Most people need glasses for reading as they grow older. If you are finding it increasingly difficult to read or to see things near you, go and have your eyes tested. You do not need a doctor's referral: just make an appointment with an ophthalmic optician or an ophthalmic medical practitioner. Regular eye examination is important not only to get a prescription for reading glasses but also because diseases can be detected, such as glaucoma, which can creep up on people without their being aware. Cataract also comes on insidiously. If, in the course of a routine sight test, any suspicious signs are found, you should be referred to your general practitioner who may send you to a specialist in the hospital eye service.

screening for cancer

A woman should take advantage of any screening for breast cancer and cervical cancer offered in her neighbourhood; it may be in community health centres or one of the regional special breast cancer screening centres. The government has instructed health authorities to set up a regular (5-yearly) screening programme up to the age of 64.

There are no screening programmes for men, but it would be prudent for men over 50 to undergo regular examination of the prostate, for the timely detection and treatment of early tumours.

Benign enlargement of the prostate is not necessarily treated unless there are troublesome symptoms, such as difficulty in passing urine.

smoking

By the time you are fifty or sixty, you are surely aware that smoking is bad for you. Even if you have been a smoker for many years, it is still worth stopping today. Cigarette smoking, even in moderation, greatly reduces the chances of enjoying a healthy retirement. When someone gives up smoking, the risk of lung disorders stops increasing and the risk of getting heart disease decreases.

A cigarette smoker runs a much greater risk of lung cancer than non-smokers do; cigarette smoking is not only associated with lung cancer, but to an even greater extent with coronary heart disease and chronic bronchitis.

chronic bronchitis and emphysema

Chronic bronchitis is a disease of the air passages in the lungs (bronchi) which become damaged and narrowed, and produce an excess of sputum (phlegm) which has to be coughed up. The characteristic symptoms of chronic bronchitis are persistent cough, producing sputum, and breathlessness.

Emphysema is a long-standing chest disease in which the lung tissue itself, rather than the bronchi, is damaged. The lung tissue is responsible for transferring oxygen from the air we breathe to the blood.

what causes chronic bronchitis and emphysema?
Both the disorders develop slowly over many years. Tobacco smoke is the main culprit in chronic bronchitis. The causes of emphysema are not clear but, without doubt, smoking is an important contributory cause. Neither chronic bronchitis nor emphysema is caused by infection nor are they infectious.

When the lungs or bronchi have been damaged they cannot be made normal again. But by stopping cigarette smoking they will at least not be made worse.

raised blood pressure

Raised blood pressure is a common problem in older people. It is important because it increases the liability to stroke and treatment will reduce this risk by about half. Unfortunately, raised blood pressure has no characteristic symptoms. It used to be thought that dizziness and flushing of the face were indicative, but this is now known to be not so. Therefore, the only way to find out is by taking a measurement of the blood pressure. This can be done conveniently by making an appointment with the practice nurse at the local medical centre or general practitioner. Sometimes, several readings may need to be taken before the doctor can decide whether and what treatment is needed. Blood pressure should be checked at least every five years.

angina

The word comes from the Greek for 'choking or strangling' but is now almost exclusively used to describe a type of heart disease.

When the arteries which supply blood to the heart muscle

(the coronary arteries) become furred up and narrowed it may result in angina. A factor bringing about a narrowing of coronary arteries is the deposit of fatty and other materials (atheroma) in the lining of the arteries. The build-up of atheroma starts in youth and is an unavoidable part of ageing. It produces no symptoms until the narrowing is far advanced. Atherosclerosis, as this degenerative process is known, can affect arteries in all parts of the body and reduces the blood supply to the affected parts. The build-up can eventually block off the blood supply altogether. When it is impossible for the blood flow to increase properly during exercise or during exertion, this can result in a tight feeling in the throat or jaw, a pressure or band-like sensation behind the breast bone, and sometimes a numbness or heaviness extending into the left arm. The feelings disappear very quickly when the exercise stops. Very similar symptoms can be produced by emotional stress such as anger, excitement, being late for an appointment.

If you experience symptoms like this, stop what you are doing, try to calm down and either stand still or, if possible, sit down for a few moments. The discomfort should rapidly disappear and you can then continue at a slower pace.

It is important that you consult your doctor about these symptoms because there are many excellent treatments which can prevent or relieve your pain and help to avoid a heart attack.

heart attacks

The usual form of heart attack occurs because one of the narrowed coronary arteries finally blocks completely and the portion of the heart muscle which received oxygen and nutrients from this artery has to die. The symptoms are very similar to those of angina except that they are usually more severe, and do not go away with rest. There is often sweating, cold clammy skin, shortness of breath and a feeling of faintness.

If this happens, try to lie down, with the upper part of the body propped up about 30°. Breathe as slowly and deeply as you can and do not take any stimulants or alcohol. A doctor should be called urgently and without delay. In some parts of the country (for example, Brighton, Belfast, Newcastle), a coronary ambulance may be available with special equipment to provide early treatment.

Remember that the first few moments after a heart attack are the most dangerous and the chances of survival improve with each hour that passes. It is often possible, in hospital, to stop progression of a heart attack or even reverse it, provided that treatment is started early. So, do not delay.

You will probably be about a week in hospital and then increase your activities gradually at home until you are fully active. The damaged portion of the heart heals into a firm scar and the undamaged muscle takes over all the work. It is helpful if you can reduce the work which the heart has to do by becoming thin, and making sure that you do not have untreated high blood pressure. There is no need to consider yourself an invalid after a heart attack. **The Chest, Heart and Stroke Association**, Tavistock House, North Tavistock Square, London WC1H 9JE (telephone 01-387 3012) has a number of relevant publications.

Bart's City life saver scheme
A scheme was set up at St. Bartholomew's Hospital, London, to train people in the techniques of CPR (cardiopulmonary resuscitation). The basic skills are easy to learn and can, if used quickly and effectively, save someone's life.

So far 10,000 people have undertaken the training and 58 have reported back that they have been able to help an accident victim or someone who was having a heart attack.

It costs £1.50 for a 2-hour session. Any individual can go

along either on a tuesday at 5 pm or thursday at 5.30 pm (you get a certificate at the end). To book, telephone 01-606 3669 – you cannot just turn up on the night.

One two-hour session will teach you how to deal with the following life- threatening emergencies:

○ how to recognise a heart attack
○ how to deal with someone who is unconscious
○ what to do if someone stops breathing
○ what to do if someone's heart stops
○ what to do if someone is bleeding severely.

Alzheimer's disease

This disease (which used to be called pre-senile dementia) may manifest itself around 65 years of age but may start as early as 45. Over 22% of people over 80 suffer from dementia in one form or another, including Alzheimer's disease. Some of the symptoms of mild dementia are a slower grasp of complex ideas, greater forgetfulness of recent events, inability to adapt to change, irritability at failure and other slight failings which may happen to people at any age. The signs of severe dementia include failure to recognise friends, relatives and everyday objects, speech not making sense. **The Alzheimer's Disease Society**, Bank Buildings, Fulham Broadway, London SW6 1ED, has published *Caring for the Person with Dementia*, a guide for families and other carers.

There is a lot of interest in the disease at present and the press have reported some promising findings about the treatment.

EMOTIONAL ASPECTS

Some people view retirement as the end of their useful life. They equate retirement with the loss of a useful occupation, money, and status and identity. They also assume that all the relationships that they have enjoyed will cease and that there will be nothing to replace them.

A major difficulty is that few people devote sufficient time and thought to their retirement. It has often been said that many years are spent preparing us for the world of work but nothing is done to prepare us to leave it. As yet, few firms offer pre-retirement courses and those that exist often concentrate on the financial aspects to the exclusion of the psychological considerations.

When facing retirement, it is natural to feel apprehensive. However much we moan about work, it does impose a set of routines and disciplines such as getting up and leaving for work. Many people also miss the status and identity given to them by a job, particularly those who see themselves as indispensable to their employer. In addition, many people miss the sense of belonging to a team as well as the feeling of comradeship which work brings.

How you view retirement affects how you will adjust. If it is seen as the end of useful life, it will soon live up to your (negative) expectations. If, however, it is seen as another life transition, involving challenge and opportunity, it is likely to be seen as a positive change.

The best way to ensure a positive attitude is to plan properly. Spending time and energy thinking about the issues involved will pay dividends. *Branching Out*, a self-teaching text published by **Lifeskills Associates**, 51 Clarendon Road, Leeds LS2 9NZ (price £10.50 plus £2 postage) contains a series of useful exercises to help people analyse their strengths and interests as well as helping them to determine what they want in the future. Taking stock in this way helps to develop self-esteem as well as helping in making important decisions such as where to live.

At all events, discussing these issues with your partner and family is important because retirement will affect them too.

immediate post-retirement blues

It is natural to feel a sense of immediate loss when leaving work for good. In order to help alleviate 'job-bereavement' it is important to go through the rituals of retirement such as the leaving party, clearing the desk and saying farewells, however tempting it might be to avoid them. Like a funeral, it fixes the fact in our minds.

Some people find it helpful to take an immediate holiday or break. Others throw themselves into a frenzy of spring cleaning, gardening or redecorating. These activities help to break the routines and provide a displacement activity. In contrast, other people take their time to adjust and use the extra time to plan a holiday properly.

If real depression or isolation strikes, it is important to seek help as soon as possible. Use friends, family, the doctor, or any of the agencies set up to provide help and support. It also goes without saying that friendships should be fostered and maintained to provide a support network and to compensate for the feeling of isolation.

In a marriage or partnership, where the man's and the woman's relative ages are such that he retires while she is still working full-time, the situation can produce special stresses. A man may be lonely and feel neglected while his wife is working, especially if his own retirement is unwelcome. He may therefore need considerable emotional support.

domestic adjustments

On a strictly practical level, it may be worth sitting down together and deciding who does what in the new regime. The man might have to learn to contribute more to the practical running of the home, now that he spends more time there. There may even be a small lesson there for a man who could not understand what his wife did all day long . . . ! However, it is unlikely that a man who has never ironed his own shirts (let alone anyone else's) will suddenly want to do so now, or find great fulfilment in doing such tasks. But vacuuming, dusting, shopping are jobs that do not require a long apprenticeship.

A man may have been holding down a responsible job for years, but not know how to cope alone in the house with a shopping list and set of instructions for the family meal. Some men are excellent cooks. There are TV cookery courses to watch, or a cookery course at the local tech, or adult education centre to attend. Some special courses are run just for men.

There may be a sudden realisation that everybody else seems to be pursuing their own goals, including the children who may now be offering advice to their father in his new role. All these situations of role-reversal call for tact and understanding on everybody's part, and it may take time to adjust.

Message to wife at retirement stage: can you change a fuse, mow the lawn and mend the lawnmower, do the decorating, turn off the mains water? Get him to teach you now – he may not be around forever. And vice versa.

women and retirement

Some of the effects of retirement are different for women than men, whether they are themselves retiring, or living with a man who is about to retire.

Where the man has retired and the wife does not go out to work, it can mean less freedom for her. A non-working wife who is used to her own routine may find it difficult to adjust to having someone around all the time. She has her own friends, her hobbies, her own way of life. Perhaps she is used to a snack lunch (or none at all) and now is expected to produce a meal every midday.

In retirement, most couples will be seeing more of each other than ever before in their married life, so what may have been a minor irritation, because they were not spending so much time together, might become a source of real friction. You may decide to grin-and-bear it; or, by putting words to a problem, it may turn out to be something trivial, after all. If it unleashes thirty years' bottled-up resentment, that, too, may be a good thing if it helps to clear the air.

It is not always appreciated that a woman's retirement from work affects her just as a man's does his. Women who resumed work after having a family or looking after a relative may particularly miss the companionship and interests outside the home, and the mental stimulation, which a job provides. A man may assume that housework will provide a woman with something to do, to fill the gap after retirement, but forgets that one of the reasons why many women have gone out to work is to prevent the housework expanding into a full-time job. She may not relish being forced to return to a life dominated by household chores.

single people
Anyone living alone may particularly miss the companionship of colleagues at work, and there may be a feeling of isolation to cope with, as well as adjustment to a life no longer centred round work. But the actual pattern of domestic life may not be all that much disrupted and, for a gregarious person, the change may not be very dramatic.

If you are single or widowed and faced with living alone in your retirement, you may need to make a special effort to get involved with your neighbours and invite friends or acquaintances home – not necessarily for a meal, but perhaps for coffee or, now that afternoons are free, for tea.

Offer your services as a babysitter and you may become the most sought-after person in the street. Perhaps do some shopping for someone who is housebound. Try to keep in contact with all age groups and, particularly, avoid falling into the trap of separating yourself from young people, even if you are mutually suspicious. If you have any expertise to offer or experience to share with young people, explore ways of becoming involved. But do not approach them with a senior-to-junior attitude: that is a recipe for disaster.

Consider inviting a student to live with you, as a paying, or non-paying guest. Contact the accommodation officer at your nearest college or university or teaching hospital. Tell him or her the type of student you would prefer: male or female, young or mature, for example, so that you will get somebody who would not be disruptive to your way of life. Many young people and mature students are serious and conscientious, some are lonely, especially overseas students. Make sure to lay down 'house rules' beforehand – about bringing in friends, music, use of kitchen, coming and going. With a bit of give-and-take, the advantages (including the financial contribution) could outweigh the disadvantages, and may in fact work out extremely well for all concerned. If not, you can always opt out next term.

working after retirement

You may need to supplement your income by finding some paid work, particularly if you have retired early, before qualifying for the state retirement pension. This may not be easy because you will be competing against much younger people, but some employers may prefer an older person. Some employers in the south east of England particularly are turning to retired people to help them cope with the skills shortage. Other employers might welcome help on a short term basis.

If you know that you will be prematurely retired, start looking as soon as possible. Use the old-boy network, use your connections through pub and club, church, old business contacts; if you do not tell people that you are available, they will not know, or be aware of the fact, that you are looking for a job. Tell your relations, neighbours, friends, acquaintances.

Use any trade or professional institutes and societies of which you may be a member; use your trade union.

The search may be long and tedious. You may have to be willing to take a job in a new field and may need to retrain. A reason for having to take early retirement may be that technology has outstripped your own knowledge and experience. So, for a new career or new occupation, consider retraining.

You can approach the Employment Training scheme (through your local jobcentre) and see what is available for you, at your age, and whether – and on what conditions – they will take you on. One condition is that you must be willing to take up employment in the occupation for which you train, but there is no guarantee of a job.

Examine what courses are on offer at your local adult education centre or technical college; the library is a good place to look for information and announcements. While looking for retraining courses, you may come across other courses or lectures that may be useful.

co-operatives

In recent years there has been a revival in small co-operatives. A co-operative is a business venture jointly owned by the people who work in it, conducted on business lines, but distributing any profits amongst its members on a democratic basis.

A co-operative may be set up under the Companies Act with a minimum of two people, or under the Industrial and Provident Societies Act with a minimum of seven people. You, too, could get together with other people and start your own co-operative. An example would be a small local gardening service with two or more people gardening and others providing back-up in book-keeping, enquiries, maintenance.

Further information, and a publications list, can be obtained from the **Co-operative Development Agency**, Broadmead House, 21 Panton Street, London SW1Y 4DR (telephone 01-839 2988). The Manchester address is Holyoake House, Hanover Street, Manchester M60 0AS (telephone 061-833 9379). How to set up a co-operative is amongst the information included in the Consumer Publication *Starting your own business*. If you have always hankered after running your own business, now might be the time to try. There are many sources of help and advice (most of it free) as well as financial support for people with a marketable idea.

possible placement agencies

Executive leasing is offered by a number of consultant or management agencies; it is a form of executive temping for managers. The leased executive is employed by the agency but works for whatever firm he or she is assigned to.

Some employment agencies which specialise in placing older people include:

Executive Stand-By Ltd, at 310 Chester Road, Hartford, Northwich CW8 2AB and **Executive Stand-By (South) Ltd**, at Office 51, 91 London Wool Exchange, Brushfield Street, London E1 6EU, and **Executive Stand-By (West) Ltd**, at Somercourt, Homefield Road, Saltford, Bristol BS18 3EG, have a register of executives who are available to fill short-term, and long-term locum management consultancy and other vacancies. They specialise in the age group 40 to 60 and do not have many calls for people over 60. With consultancy jobs, however, their clients are not so concerned about the age if people have the necessary expertise.

Intex Executives (UK) Ltd, Chancery House, 53–64 Chancery Lane, London WC2A 1QU provides senior executives, managers or technicians, to employers, on a short or variable term full or part-time basis.

Success After Sixty, 40–41 Old Bond Street, London W1X 3AF is an employment agency which will introduce to employers people over 50 who are looking for part-time or full-time employment in the London area.

P.A.M. Personnel, 68 Shaftesbury Avenue London W1V 7DF, is an employment agency with a special 'over 40' section which was started in the belief that people within this bracket have a lot to offer in the way of reliability, experience and loyalty. This section was started by someone who is herself the other side of 40.

Part-Time Careers Ltd, 10 Golden Square, London W1R 3AF specialise in finding part-time openings, mostly in the London area, including placements for retired and redundant people (mainly accountants and bookkeepers).

Homesitters, The Old Bakery, Wester Road, Tring, Herts HP23 4BB, is a house-sitting agency employing older people to live temporarily in a house or flat which would otherwise be standing empty (owners on holiday, cats to feed, plants to water, dogs to walk). Applicants must be over 40 years and available to be considered for assignments for a minimum of 12 weeks spread throughout the year.

Housewatch Ltd, Barleycroft, Little London, Berdon, Bishop's Stortford, Herts CM23 1BE, is a similar organisation supplying occupants for absentees such as owners gone abroad, death in the family, making sure household insurance is not invalidated by the house being empty for longer than the stated period. People over 50 are positively preferred. The job is part-time, varied, requires initiative and gets you out of your own house. It is, however, to be treated as a job, not a holiday.

Buretire (UK) Ltd, run by **The Age Endeavour Fellowship**, Willowthorpe, High Street, Stanstead Abbotts, Herts SG12 8AS, is a charity concerned with employment and activity in retirement. The employment bureau aims to find part-time employment for newly-retired and disabled people.

The Emeritus Register is a scheme to link retired former employees of a number of large firms, who are still keen to work, with businesses and organisations seeking part-time or short-term help. It covers both voluntary and paid employment.

Only pensioners of firms who are in the scheme can participate; it is up to firms to join the scheme for the benefit of their own future ex-employee pensioners. Employers who are interested should get in touch with the administrator of the scheme at 1st floor, Quadrant Arcade Chambers, Romford RM1 3EH.

the earnings rule

If you are past retirement age, remember the 'earnings rule': you lose 5p of basic pension for every 10p you earn over £75 a week up to £79, and 5p for every 5p (that is, pound for pond) earned over £79. (These figures are periodically updated.) And anything you earn may affect the amount of tax you have to pay. So you may find that to make it worthwhile, you would have to earn a high salary or fee, perhaps higher than you can demand.

Your earnings count for the week in which they are earned, even if you do not receive them until later. If you do not know in advance how much you will earn, your pension may be reduced in line with an estimate of what your earnings might be, and will then be adjusted when the final amount is known.

occasional jobs, freelance work

A person who has retired may want to find work not just for financial reasons but for personal ones, such as getting out of the house, companionship, involvement. Even in today's economic climate there are employers who may be glad of someone who is willing to work for, say, two or three hours a day, or one day a week, earning just within the limit of the earnings rule.

There may be seasonal jobs for a retired accountant to prepare small firm's books, for an ex-civil servant to advise on form-filling; someone to man the office when all the workmen (boss included) are out on jobs; a handyman to do an accumulation of repairs in, or decorate the outside of, a house, or do odd-job gardening.

Employers know how much retired people can earn without their pensions being affected. The remuneration can often be tailored to fit the pensioner's free limits, but beware of being exploited. It may be tempting to accept cash-in-hand payment, but it is probably better to insist on the rate for the job and be ready to pay tax on it.

It may be difficult to obtain even part-time employment on a reasonable salary, but it is quite possible that voluntary or 'expenses-only' work can be found – possibly more than one job. Voluntary jobs, although not offering a salary or pay, may cover travelling expenses (and give you the opportunity to travel – even if it is only to the other end of town), and expenses such as postage and telephone calls.

Telephone calls, even if they are strictly for business purposes, mean that you have to be in communication with outsiders: a defence against the isolation that some people fear in retirement.

help exchanges

Exchanging help for help is not a new concept and good neighbours have been doing it since time immemorial.

Often people who do not fall into any particular category of great need would like a little help from time to time – with the garden, income tax returns, redecorating, shortening the sleeves of a jacket, seeing what is wrong with the car – and yet are unable to pay much (or anything) for it because they are retired people living on a limited income. It would only take a few retired people living in the same area to set up a bank of skills, offering one hour of a skill in exchange for an hour of any other skill. Self-help groups need not be restricted to retired people. An exchange of skills on a time basis could extend to every member in a community and all age groups.

voluntary work

Many people do voluntary work in a limited way without really considering it as voluntary work – that is, by helping neighbours in the community. After retirement, with more leisure, it is possible to do so in a somewhat more organised way. In some respects, voluntary work can offer some of the bonuses that employment gave you: company, outside involvement, a sense of personal value and an up-to-date reference, which should be particularly useful if you decide to try a part-time return to paid work in the future.

There are many voluntary organisations, and in every sphere there is always demand for volunteers, not only for the large national organisations, but in local ones – for example, local housing organisations, local hospital, charity shop. **The Age Endeavour Fellowship** runs activity centres to enable people to use their skills and maintain contact with other people. They always need volunteers.

To find voluntary work, you might also start by contacting your local authority's social services department regarding:

- meals on wheels
- visiting the house-bound
- visiting the hospital-bound
- hosting at an old people's club
- assisting the youth officer at a young people's club
- preservation of public footpaths (this may come under the technical services department of the local authority).

The public library may have information about local societies (or you might start a group, if there is none) concerned with environmental matters, pollution of air, soil and streams; disappearance of hedges; threatened closure of branch railway line or rural bus service.

Contact the volunteer coordinator at your regional office of the **National Trust** (see local telephone directory) or write to Assistant Secretary (Volunteers), 36 Queen Anne's Gate, London SW1H 9AS about opportunities to help at local Trust properties – houses and open spaces – or in a growing range of office and specialised tasks such as photography, lecturing, archive collection.

Many museums need volunteers to man the information desk or act as guides.

Retired Executive Action Clearing House (REACH), 89 Southwark Street, London SE1 0HD (telephone 01-928 0452) links retired executives to useful part-time work with voluntary organisations on an expenses-only basis, making use of the skills and experience acquired during their working life. The publication *Work after Work*, by Judy Kirby (£2.95) available in bookshops, is an account of the opportunities for voluntary activities, such as REACH fosters.

Anyone interested in voluntary work should contact their local volunteer bureau or council for voluntary service (or, in country areas, community council or council of community service). These will be listed in Yellow Pages under social service and welfare organisations. Details of volunteer bureaux or of councils for voluntary service or of community councils can be obtained from the **National Council for Voluntary Organisations**, 26 Bedford Square, London WC1B 3HU (telephone 01-636 4066), who publish a full directory of voluntary groups (£7.95).

There are even opportunities for working abroad with VSO (**Voluntary Service Overseas**) and related organisations. VSO accepts volunteers up to the age of 65, with appropriate work experience and qualifications, in good health and able to spend at least 2 years overseas working for payment based on local rates.

enjoy it

In paid employment, people usually have some idea of the hours they will work, the type of work they would like to do and the money they would like to earn. Some of the same considerations apply to voluntary work, so be prepared to ask about them at any voluntary workers' bureau. Make sure that, if you are going to do voluntary work, you will not be out of pocket: if you are offering your services free, do not hesitate to ask if your expenses will be covered.

Many of us have to spend our working lives doing jobs we are not particularly keen on because we need the money, but this is not a consideration with voluntary work in retirement. Most voluntary organisations have a variety of jobs on offer, and skills needed. Think what skills you have to offer (and want to offer) before deciding to contact any organisation.

Do something which you are going to enjoy because there is little point in doing voluntary work unless you are going to get some satisfaction from it. If the smell of hospitals makes you feel upset or uneasy, there is no point in going to do voluntary work in a hospital. If you do not care for children, then working with them would be a mistake. If you are put on 'fund raising' and find this uncongenial, ask for an alternative job – say office work or something within the scope of your capabilities which you will be happy and comfortable doing.

If you have been dissatisfied with the job you have been doing for the last ten or twenty or more years, and been eagerly awaiting retirement, think carefully before going back to doing the same thing – without the pay.

An important consideration before offering yourself for voluntary work is how much time you really want to give. When you have quite a lot of free time, you may want to be very generous with it. But voluntary work snowballs: if you have not had any experience of it, a good idea is to offer a couple of hours to begin with, and then do more if you enjoy it and find that it is not going to encroach too much on your freedom. Sometimes volunteers deal with people who become very dependent, so that it is difficult to resist demands - until the 'two hours' develops into four or more.

On the other hand, we all like to feel that we are needed and voluntary work can give a great deal of satisfaction.

HELP IN MAKING ENDS MEET

You may think that you are too well-off to qualify for any help, but if you find it difficult to make ends meet, make sure you know what you are entitled to, by checking with your local social security office or the social services department at your town hall.

family credit
Anyone who works for at least 24 hours a week, whose income is below a certain statutory minimum and has at least one child living at home who is under the age of 16 (or over 16 but under 19 and still at school) can apply for family credit. Leaflet FC1, available from social security offices and post offices, gives full details and a claim form.

Children are the qualifying factor, but someone forced to retire at, say, 58 may well still have a school-age child, particularly of a second marriage.

income support
A person over the state retirement age, who is not in paid full-time work (if working, does so for less than 24 hours a week), and whose resources are less than his or her requirements (both resources and requirements according to official definitions), may qualify for income support; this is not dependent in any way on the number of NI contributions a person has made. To be eligible, your savings and investments must not be more than £6,000, the net income must be less than a set figure, which depends on whether you are a single person or a married couple and on some other factors. The income support is not taxable.

Leaflet SB1, available from local social security offices or post offices, gives you details and a claim form. (It is proposed that income support paid to pensioners will be restructured from October 1989.)

You will have to give particulars of all your income, and other detailed information. You can choose to have a personal interview with someone from the social security office either in your own home or at the social security office.

income support extras

If you are responsible for paying housing costs you may be able to get help from income support or from housing benefit; the amount depends on the size of the family, and the amount of rent or rates payable. Application has to be made to the housing department of the local authority. Form RR1 which you can get from the local social security office gives details.

If you have a low income or claim income support, you may be able to claim help with fares to and from hospital. Get leaflet H11 for further information.

Someone getting income support who needs glasses will get a voucher to use in payment for the spectacles, and so may someone with a low income only just above income support level. Leaflet AB11 gives details.

Dental treatment is free if you are receiving income support (make sure you tell your dentist, and ask him for form F1D); you may also qualify for free treatment or help with charges if your income is low. Get leaflet D11 for details.

cold weather payments

A small cash payment is available to anyone over the age of 60 in receipt of income support to pay towards heating bills during any very cold spells. The payment is £5 for each week of very cold weather. People who make a successful claim in respect of one period of very cold weather will automatically receive payments for later periods in the same winter.

the telephone

Telephone payments can be spread over the year by buying telephone stamps at the post office at regular intervals, or through a monthly direct debit based on average usage.

If you have a rented phone and make few calls, you may be able to take advantage of the 'low user' rental rebate. On lines rented at the residential rate, where the number of call units per quarter is less than 120, a rebate of 3.6p is given for each unused unit below 120.

thinking about the car

If you have a car, you might consider getting rid of it (which will bring a small lump sum and save running costs). Amongst the advantages of having a car are the sheer convenience, not having to wait for public transport in wet and draughty conditions and not having to be exposed to colds and germs when travelling in crowded public vehicles. A car is invaluable when a necessary visit to the doctor has to be made. A car is, however, a major expense: insurance, vehicle licence tax, MOT test, are basic costs even if you drive only to the shopping centre once a week. To this has to be added the cost of petrol and oil, parking fees, servicing and repairs, depreciation (that is, how much less the car will be worth if and when you sell it). To save on costs, think about

○ changing to a car that uses less and cheaper petrol
○ changing to a car in a low insurance group (you may be able to reduce the insurance premium by taking what is known as an excess, that is being willing to pay part of any claim – say £50 – yourself)
○ learning about car maintenance and doing some of it yourself which can save garage bills
○ sharing some journeys and cost with a neighbour by using the car jointly or on set alternate dates (but that may lead to the end of a long friendship).

A couple who rely on a car for transport should make sure that both people can drive: it may be necessary in an emergency, and useful in everyday circumstances.

In a two-car family, giving up one of the two would save a lot of money and make economic sense, but be sure you think it through and talk it over first.

driving licence

The **Driver and Vehicle Licensing Centre** (DVLC) will normally send you a reminder to renew your licence about five weeks before it expires on your 70th birthday, so it is important to notify any change of address by completing the back of your licence with your new address and sending it to DVLC, Swansea SA99 1BN. Alternatively, you can get a renewal form D1 from any post office.

After 70, the licence can be renewed for three years, and then again for three years, and so on. On an application for a driving licence, details must be included of any physical or mental disabilities which may affect your ability to drive safely.

Further information on the type of disability to be declared can be found on form D100 obtainable from post offices.

If an entry on the form alerts the DVLC to the possible need for a medical examination, they send the form to their medical section who will ask you to complete a medical questionnaire and give consent for them to obtain a report from your GP. Depending on the information given by you on the questionnaire, they may require you to be examined by a local medical officer. The cost of the report is paid for by the DVLC but you will have to pay any travelling expenses.

It is possible that you will then be issued with a medically restricted licence. The medical restriction might be in terms of time, for example a licence issued for only one year or two years where the disability is progressive, or restricted to a type of vehicle, for example, a motor car with controls which can be correctly and conveniently operated by you.

Some insurance companies ask for a medical certificate every year after the age of 70 (or 73, or 75), before renewing the policy. The driver has to pay for the certificate. The fee recommended by the British Medical Association for a medical certificate is £25, but many doctors charge less in recognition of the applicant's limited means.

giving up the car?

If you drive less than about 4000 miles a year, it can be cheaper to hire a car occasionally rather than own one. This does not take into account the convenience of being able to step into your own car whenever you wish. And remember that if you hire a self-drive car, it has to be collected and returned to what may be an inconvenient point. Also, you will be driving only now and then and using an unfamiliar car.

Quite apart from the saving by not having a car, you would no longer have to cope with the general hassle of driving, which will become more irritating as you get older. But do not give up your car lightly if you think that being without one would leave you isolated.

using your home to raise capital or income

For most homeowners, the home is likely to be their main capital asset, often indeed the only capital asset of significance. When you stop working, the change to drawing a pension will almost certainly mean a reduction in income. There is also the risk that the real value of both capital and income may be gradually eroded by the effect of inflation.

But retirement can also bring changes for the better to your capital position. For instance, a lump sum from your pension fund may give you the chance to consider repaying your mortgage. You may perhaps find yourself at liberty to move 'down market' to a less expensive home and invest the difference in price between the two properties to augment your income.

At retirement age, a lot of capital is likely to be locked up in your home. This will only be perceived as a problem if you have difficulty in making ends meet out of income. It is a problem that can be resolved in a variety of ways.

raising an income through home income plans

Lesser mortals can only claim income tax relief for interest on loans up to £30,000 used to buy a home. Pensioners, for once, have an advantage. They are allowed relief on loans raised on a property which they already own for the purpose of entering into a mortgage annuity scheme, better known as a home income plan.

Home income plans are based on your owning a property (without mortgages), and using the equity in it (that is, its worth) as security for a loan. The transaction is carried out through a financial institution operating a home income plan, such as a building society or a life insurance company.

The lump sum you borrow (minus an administration fee) is used to buy an annuity, that is a fixed income which will be paid to you, for the rest of your life. The older you are, the greater the annuity will be since it is calculated on the basis of your life expectancy. Part of the annuity income pays the interest on the loan on which there is tax relief. The rest of the income comes to you, until you die.

Most companies insist on a minimum age of 70. For a couple, both would have to be over this age, generally with a combined age of 150. Obviously, the older you are, the better an annuity income you are likely to be able to buy. It would be wise to have the house in joint names and make the annuity a 'second death' or 'last survivor' one. The annuity income for a single person is higher than for a couple where the annuity runs until the second person dies. Annuity rates – like pensions – are also determined by the interest rate prevailing at the time when the annuity is bought. With a fixed-interest scheme, later changes in interest rates do not affect the annuity. With a variable-interest loan, your income goes down if rates go up.

Under home income schemes it is possible to go back to the annuity company for another bite at the cherry. Suppose you borrowed £30,000 five years ago when your house was worth £40,000. Inflation has now pushed its value up to £80,000. There is now an equity of £50,000 in the house and you should be able to borrow up to at least another £30,000. The new annuity should be rather better than the original one (you are five years older). But there is no tax relief because the £30,000 ceiling was reached before the extra loan.

The loan will have to be repaid on death or, in the case of a married couple, on the death of the survivor. The value of the estate will be reduced by the loan repayment, but if inheritance tax would have been payable on that sum, the loss to the estate is considerably diminished. A home income scheme can form part of a strategy to reduce the burden of inheritance tax.

These schemes can prove disadvantageous to people receiving means-tested social security benefits such as income support or housing benefit. They should only be considered if they bring a significant increase in net income after taking account of any loss of state benefits.

There are other points to bear in mind:

○ The annuity income is essentially static, but interest rates (payable on the loan) vary. So your net income could rise or fall if the interest rate changes.

○ If you were to buy an annuity but die shortly afterwards, the capital would, of course, be lost forever. It is possible to implement a scheme which guarantees repayment of the capital if you die within a specified period. This has its cost, in terms of a reduced income. Or you might consider taking out a separate life policy to cover this possibility.

○ Some home income plans will allow you to take part of the loan as a cash sum (the maximum being 10%).

home income plans and moving home

If you move home after having a home income plan – selling one house to buy another – you will probably have two options. Firstly, you could repay the loan. In this case you will retain the annuity income, indeed it will increase (in real terms) because none of it will now be diverted to paying interest on the loan. But if you are buying another home, you could also try to negotiate with the annuity company to switch the loan over to the new property. Depending on the value of the new home, you might have to repay part of the loan. If you are considering a home income scheme, make sure to ask what criteria the company would apply to switching the loan if you were to move home.

If you are selling your home but not buying another one, you have no option but to repay the loan.

raising capital through home reversion schemes

Home reversion schemes work like this: you part with the ownership of your home in return for a capital sum coupled with the right to continue living there for life. The lump sum is not the full value of the house, generally no more than 50% of it, or as little as 20% depending on your age at the time (minimum usually 70) and the financial institution concerned. Rates and repairs remain your responsibility and there is a small ground rent payable.

Entering a home reversion scheme is a final and indeed irrevocable step to take. It is unlikely to be appropriate except in very unusual circumstances. Most retired people will be more concerned to ensure they have an adequate income than to raise a large capital sum.

home reversion schemes – variants

There are of course variants of home reversion schemes. One such, available for purchasers from some sheltered housing developments, enables you in effect to buy a discounted life share in a flat or house, and could make a significant difference to the housing available to you. For example, £50,000 might be your contribution towards a property costing £100,000. The balance would come from the company administering the scheme. You do not receive a capital sum in your own hands, nor an income, nor do you own the property (you lease it from the company for life) and on your death, your inheritors get nothing.

Another variant enables you to sell in return for an annuity, i.e. an income for life, coupled with the right to live there for life. The income in your hands would be superior to that released by the same capital sum under a home income plan, since you do not have to make any interest payments. Under some schemes, the annuity figure is adjusted annually as all houses in the scheme are regularly valued.

Under yet another variant, you can retain a percentage of the capital value of the house.

Other points to bear in mind about home reversion schemes:

○ If you no longer own your home, you are losing the benefit of any increase in its value under most schemes. Contrast this with home income plans, where you can often use an increase in value to raise another annuity.
○ If you need to move home, you could have problems. For a start, you will be abandoning the guaranteed right to live there for life. You have already sold your home, so you would have to find the capital to buy another one. You should therefore make sure that you find out exactly what options you have (if any) to renegotiate the scheme if you move.

○ There are no income tax advantages. (Admittedly, those available for home income plans are hardly earth-shattering, but they often make them viable financially).
○ As with home income plans, check whether any state benefits are likely to be lost.

home income and home reversion schemes – a final word

Both these schemes can mean a significant reduction in the value of your estate on death. Under a home reversion scheme, the home will not be yours to leave by will; a home income scheme may mean that the home will eventually have to be sold in order to repay the loan. So if there are any beneficiaries under your will, it may be worth telling them before you take the plunge.

You would in any case be well advised to seek independent financial advice before you go ahead. The *Which?* update report on investments for older people published in August 1987 says, "we do not recommend part-reversionary or reversionary schemes which involve an immediate sale of part or the whole of your home."

putting affairs in order

Some people have their affairs in order all the time, but for those who have not, the run-up to retirement or perhaps immediately after they have retired, with more time on their hands, is a good opportunity to sit down and take stock. For people who are planning to move house, there may be a need to sort things out, to throw out old papers and clobber and be forced to get themselves well and truly organised.

Both partners should know where important documents are kept, insurance policy for house, car, life insurance, deeds to property, share certificates, and so on.

A person living alone who, in an emergency, would be dependent on neighbours, should have placed in some obvious position the telephone number and address of a close friend or relative who could be contacted.

have you made a will?

Making a will does not mean that you are going to die one minute earlier; not making a will may well mean that your possessions, after death, will go to someone to whom in life you would not have given them. You may think that it will all go to your wife/husband anyway – but whether it will depends on how much the 'all' is, and whether there are any surviving children or possibly surviving parents. Your spouse may die before you, anyway. The Consumer Publication *Wills and probate* sets out clearly what happens to the possessions of a person who dies intestate (that is, without having made a will) and describes what is involved in making a will. There is also an action-pack *Make Your Will* (£6.95) with charts, forms and worksheets.

considering inheritance tax

One important matter to bear in mind when making a will is that inheritance tax (IHT) affects transfers of property on death, that is gifts, legacies and bequests, and certain transfers within seven years before the date of death. However, there are some exemptions from IHT; the most relevant of them is that each year a person can give away £3,000 without tax; that on death, no IHT is payable on (at present) £110,000, and that all property passing from husband to wife (or vice versa) on death is wholly exempt from inheritance tax. This is an advantage if you plan to leave it all to your wife/husband. But bear in mind that tax will then have to be paid when she or he dies. So it is worth considering, all other things being equal, to make lifetime gifts to children in the hope that you will live on for a further seven years, and in your will use up some of the tax-free allowance in favour of, say, children.

Another exemption from inheritance tax is a gift to charity or to a political party. If you leave something to a charity in your will, the amount will be deducted from your total estate (which may then possibly be reduced to below the IHT threshold). It is important to get the name of the charity correct and to put a clause into the will about a receipt from the proper officer of the charity.

appointing executors

It is usual to appoint executors, in a will. An executor is the person whose responsibility it will be to see that the wishes expressed in the will are carried out. To do so, the executor of a will has to obtain a grant of probate (which involves a certain amount of paperwork and calculations), pay the IHT (not out of his own pocket, but he has to make the arrangements for the payment), pay off the debts of the person who has died, and make sure everything is perfectly in order, before distributing the property to the people who are to benefit from the wishes expressed in the will (the beneficiaries).

It is a responsible, time-consuming job, even when everything is quite straightforward. Often two people are appointed to be executors, to share the burden. It is a good idea to appoint as executors one or more of the main beneficiaries who have a stake in seeing that the administration is carried out as smoothly as possible. Or appoint as the second executor a friend or relative who is a professional person or is used to dealing with paperwork.

If a solicitor or accountant is appointed in his professional capacity, a clause is usually put into the will allowing him or her to charge a professional fee. In other cases, it is customary to leave a small legacy to the executor who is not otherwise a beneficiary.

Although it is not binding on the person who is named in a will to act as executor when the time comes, it is best to ask first, before making the appointment, so as to give the person a chance to say 'no' and to let somebody else be appointed.

Instructions for my next-of-kin and executors, available from **Age Concern England** (Bernard Sunley House, 60 Pitcairn Road, Mitcham, Surrey CR4 3LL, price 25p) is a useful 4-page form on which to fill in detailed personal financial information that will help executors when the time comes for them to act.

As one grows older, it is inevitable that certain friends and relatives will die. (That is why it is generally wise to choose executors who are younger than you.) There is no need to avoid discussion of the subject. For instance, if someone you care for feels strongly about, say, cremation or formal rites, it is right that you should know – and vice versa.

Review your will every so often – when there has been a change in what you own (perhaps after selling your house) or if one of the intended legatees dies. And remember, if you get married, a marriage automatically revokes the will.

power of attorney

Many people who are themselves at retirement age have elderly relatives who may be finding it increasingly difficult to look after their own affairs. It may be advisable discussing with them the question of giving you their power of attorney.

A power of attorney is a document which gives one person authority to act on behalf of another. It need not necessarily be used immediately, perhaps never. The elderly relatives should continue to be in charge of their own affairs as they were before. But in the event of, perhaps, a stroke or something which prevents them from writing or dealing with official papers or the bank, for instance, the power of attorney is there to be used.

It is possible to limit the power of attorney in any way the donor sees fit but unless any limitation is placed on the attorney's power in the document, the donor should realise that the donee can use the power of attorney for any purpose – including the making of gifts to himself or herself.

Until 1986, the ability of one person to deal with another's affairs under a power of attorney was limited by several factors. A separate power of attorney was needed for dealing with a person's own personal affairs and dealing with his affairs as trustee.

Even a general power of attorney became revoked as soon as the donor ceased to have the full mental capacity which would have been necessary to sign the relevant document himself. The only way of dealing with such a person's affairs was the extremely complicated and expensive method of appointing a receiver through the Court of Protection.

the difference now
Under the Enduring Powers of Attorney Act 1985, it is now possible for a donor (that is, the person giving power of

attorney to someone else) to execute a power of attorney both for trusts and for other matters, and with a view that the power of attorney should 'endure' through any intervening incapacity of the donor. This can therefore obviate the need for the appointment of a receiver through the Court of Protection.

The enduring power of attorney must be executed by the donor and donee on the designated form (obtainable through law stationers). Until any incapacity, it will operate in the same way as a general trust power of attorney would have operated. Should the donor then become incapacitated, the power of attorney ceases in the same way as it used to. However, the difference is that the power of attorney can now be resurrected without application through the Court of Protection simply by registration in the Court of Protection, after certain formalities have been strictly complied with.

All the official forms required are obtainable through law stationers. The power of attorney itself must be executed by the donee as well as the donor in the presence of a witness who must then add his signature, name and address and occupation.

on incapacity
As soon as the donee has reason to believe that the donor is, or is becoming, mentally incapable he must make an application for registration of the power of attorney in the Court of Protection. Before doing so, notice must be given to relatives of the donor in a specified order.

The requirements as to notice and forms and fee payable must be strictly adhered to; there will probably be a short period, of up to six weeks or so, when the registration formalities are being gone through, during which the attorney should not use the power of attorney.

Once the power has been registered, the attorney may proceed to use the power of attorney as before and can sign letters of instruction on behalf of the donor, deal with any matters relating to any bank account of the donor and sign any documents relating to sales of stocks and shares and land.

getting advice

In all situations where you may need explanations about official documents, or need help and advice generally on any official or legal or administrative matter, or want to ask questions about pensions, the local citizens advice bureau might be able to help.

If necessary, you can find out the address of your nearest **citizens advice bureau** by getting in touch with the registry department of NACAB, Myddleton House, 115 Pentonville Road, London N1 9LZ (telephone 01-833 2181).

INVESTMENTS

Financial planning for retirement is important. For some people, getting it right will allow them a comfortable lifestyle with holidays and running a car, which otherwise might not be possible. The first decisions should have been taken as early as the late teens or early twenties when a person decides whether or not to join a pension scheme. For the majority of people, pension will constitute the bulk of their income, whether provided by the state, by an employer or by a personal or self-employed scheme they have set up themselves. (This subject is covered in the chapter on pensions.)

In any event, it is never too early to supplement pension contributions either by means of additional voluntary contributions or by buying additional years (for someone in an appropriate scheme, such as the teachers' superannuation scheme or civil service schemes). This should be done as early as possible if it can be afforded: the earlier this is done, the more the compounding effect and better the value for money obtained. A very few years prior to retirement will obtain very little in investment value because of the limited time scale.

saving to invest

When questions of pension payments have been sorted out, that is the time to consider saving in an organised manner to improve one's income (and therefore lifestyle) in retirement.

It is important to formulate a plan because it is difficult to save or invest in a haphazard way. Everyone can benefit from this. Sadly, one still hears of old people who have kept their life savings under the mattress and then been burgled – and even if not burgled, inflation has eroded the savings.

Most people will not be able to afford to save for retirement until their children are grown up and off their hands, mainly when they are in their forties and fifties. It may well be the first time that they have been in the happy situation of having money available for investment.

planning ten years or more before retirement

Before entering into any kind of savings scheme it is always wise to have a contingency fund for such emergencies as urgent house repairs, or any of the other misfortunes that can befall us. Many people think that this fund should be equivalent to approximately three months' earnings, but that is only a rule of thumb. If this fund has not been established, now is the time to build it up. The obvious place for this will be an easy-access bank or building society investment account, for basic rate tax payers.

Once an emergency fund has been established, long-term savings schemes can be considered. The longer the term available, the greater element of risk can be considered because time tends to iron out risks. However, whatever scheme is undertaken, it is important to ensure that payments can be kept up, because there are nearly always financial penalties for stopping schemes before their full term. Provided that this condition can be met, some of the alternatives are

Life insurance savings schemes (which are usually for a minimum of ten years). They include with-profit endowment policies and unit-linked life insurance. Endowments can only go up in value, although not by guaranteed amounts; the value of units can go up and down and they are therefore riskier. Whole-life policies, either unit-linked, or with-profits, can be considered. Although these are primarily for protection of your dependants in case of your death, they can also contain a savings element; if you take out a with-profits endowment policy and you survive to the end of the term, you get the sum assured plus all the bonuses which have accrued for the full term. If you die during the term of the policy, your estate (or the beneficiaries if you have placed the policy in trust), get the sum assured plus the bonuses to the date of death, for unit-linked, the amount will depend on the value of the units, which fluctuate with the market.

Unit-linked is an expression meaning life insurance policies linked to units rather than with-profits. Unit trusts have no life insurance element and unit trust savings schemes do not have life insurance.

Unit trust saving schemes can produce high growth, particularly over a long period of time, but are risky because the value of the money invested can go down instead of up.

Friendly society bonds are well worth considering (although they carry the same sort of risk factor as unit trusts) because no tax is payable either by the investor or the company. There are very strict limits on the amount which may be invested, currently £9 per month (but spouses can each invest £9). They must be considered as an investment for 10 years minimum; a government restriction to prevent abuse of the system is that if you cash them in under 10 years, you only get your money back.

National Savings certificates give an unspectacular return, except for higher rate tax payers, but are safe. The index-linked variety could prove to be a winner if inflation takes off again.

British government stocks, known as 'gilts': a guaranteed return is assured and it is certainly worth looking for new issues maturing when you are likely to need your money back. Unfortunately, many of the already issued stocks are standing above their issue price and consequently, although the yield can be good, the investor will be forced to take a capital loss when they are redeemed on maturing. There are some index-linked gilts available which are well worth looking at particularly for higher rate tax payers, because gilts are free of capital gains tax. Index-linked ones have a low yield, therefore higher rate taxpayers do not get a lot of unwanted income but do get a gain which is tax free. Gilts are less suitable for regular investment; although it is possible to invest regularly in gilts it is not really cost effective unless done through National Savings Stock Register where no commission is payable. But there are unit trusts which specialise in gilts, which often have monthly saving schemes available.

planning four or five years before retirement

It is still possible to make additional voluntary contributions to your pension scheme at this stage, although ideally this should have been started earlier on. People in appropriate government schemes may still buy extra years. It will be necessary to obtain a quotation (which can take many months from some pension trustees). Seek independent advice as to whether free-standing AVCs would be more worthwhile (that is, contributions to a scheme outside your employer's scheme, run by a pension provider such as an insurance company. On the whole, free-standing AVCs do not offer such good value because the expense of setting up the scheme and possibly commission would have to be borne by you – as against an employer's AVC scheme).

For other investments, safety is of the prime importance because time is short and if things went wrong there would not be time for recovery. Risk should be kept to a minimum and for someone contributing to a private pension scheme, now is the time to switch out of equity funds and into index-linked or fixed interest ones. This is particularly true if the stock exchange is at a high level.

Now is the latest time for investing in National Savings with an initial maturity date at retirement, because they usually run for five years. Building society and bank deposit accounts will, of course, continue to be suitable and so will British government stocks with a suitable maturity date. Index-linked investments will also be appropriate.

planning a year or so before retirement

The choice of savings methods is now really restricted to investments which are easily encashed, such as building society and bank deposit accounts. There may still just be time to top up pension arrangements.

planning when you retire

It is essential to draw up a likely budget because, obviously, in even the best pension schemes, your income is going to be reduced by a third.

Shortly before retirement, you should have heard from whatever pension scheme you are in; if not, now is the time to contact them to clarify the amount that will be available as a lump sum.

Apart from the pension, lump sums may come from selling your house and moving into a cheaper one or from other sources. For example, there may be investments maturing about now, such as life policies and savings schemes arranged earlier. However, if the markets are low, not all (or, if you can afford it, none) of these should be realised but allowed to run, if this is possible.

spending the lump sum, or part of it

Where there is still an outstanding mortgage debt, consideration should be given to whether this should be kept going or paid off from some of the lump sum available.

For someone who has to give up a company car, part of the money may be needed to buy a vehicle – remember to shop around for a good deal for car insurance.

Some people use part of their lump sums to have the holiday of a lifetime, such as a cruise or visiting relations on the other side of the world. Others may like to improve their house or garden or buy consumer goods which could not be afforded previously. Perhaps this is a good moment for improving the insulation of the property; an effective central heating system would be another idea.

investing the lump sum

In most cases, the bulk of the lump sum will be a means of supplementing the pension, and/or providing a nest egg for emergencies in the future. For many people it may well be the largest sum of money that they have ever owned. While this is an exciting prospect, it is also essential to treat it sensibly.

If the entire sum is put into the building society, in twenty years' time, assuming inflation at 5%, the capital will have more than halved in value (even if the interest payments keep up with inflation) which is a sobering thought.

getting advice

There are alternatives, all of which have a degree of risk. It is therefore necessary to weigh up the pros and cons and to take advice. Many people are more than willing to provide this advice; they include the following:

Bank managers – they may be either tied agents (that is, giving advice only about own products) or independent (that is, giving advice on all the available products – life insurance, unit trusts etc.) A specialised investment department of a bank will almost certainly be a better bet when seeking advice.

Accountant – he will need to be authorised to give investment advice and you should choose one who specialises in this. You can check with the body he says authorises him; it should be specified on his notepaper.

Building society – may be tied or independent, and the expertise may vary.

Investment advisers – independent ones will be authorised by one of the self-regulatory organisations such as FIMBRA (which stands for the Financial Intermediaries Managers and Brokers Regulatory Association) or IMRO (the Investment Management Regulatory Organisation) and tied ones must say which insurance company they are representing.

Solicitors – the ones who are allowed to give investment advice are authorised by their recognised professional body (the Law Society), and this fact will be stated on their notepaper. Many firms now have financial experts working for them; it is essential to find a firm which specialises in this type of business.

The investment of this lump sum is so important that a cautious person should seek at least two opinions. Even if the investments are recommended by an adviser, remember the following guidelines:

○ Use only reputable insurance companies, they will usually be household names and will belong to LAUTRO (Life Assurance and Unit Trust Regulatory Organisation, one of the self-regulating organisations under the Securities and Investment Board)
○ Unit trust companies have to be regulated by LAUTRO and are usually members of the Unit Trust Association although there are some reputable firms who are not. In any event your money is looked after by a trustee and the prices are readily checked in the financial press.
○ Do not be tempted by wonderful, spectacular offers made by unknown firms.

what you can get from investment

The different types of investment differ in the amount of income they produce (the return), how often it is paid, whether they can fluctuate in value, how they affect your tax position, and the arrangements for getting your money back again. Last and not least is the safety aspect.

the return

There are two major reasons for investment, the first is to obtain the maximum current income commensurate with security, and the second is to make the capital grow either while receiving a reduced income or by foregoing this altogether. Income comes in two forms: interest and dividends. Some investments allow you to 'roll up' the income, that is, add it to your investment and get further interest on the compounded amount and later on take it as capital. With some investments this will continue to be taxed as income rather than as a capital gain. With some investments, you can cash in part of the capital as it grows and spend the proceeds as income.

how often it is paid
Most investment income is paid regularly – annually, half-yearly, quarterly or monthly depending on the type of investment. If investing in accounts that pay out annually, it is worth spreading your investment over four different payers so that the income does not all arrive at one particular time of year, which can be inconvenient. Before investing, find out when the dividend or interest is paid. Bear in mind that annual payments give you a lower rate of return because the interest is payable in arrears and therefore the company has had the use of the money for longer and you for shorter.

fluctuation in the value, and risk

Even leaving money in a bank or building society carries a degree of risk, for two reasons. One is that the amount of income paid can be lower than inflation; this has been the case for the majority of the past twenty years or so. Secondly, the same inflation will erode the value of the capital as time goes by. A risk-free investment which keeps up with inflation is either index-linked National Savings certificates which pay no income, or index-linked gilts which pay a very small but increasing income. (Incidentally, both of them are excellent investments for higher rate taxpayers.) The only way of hoping to keep ahead of inflation is by investing in so-called assets-backed investments, such as unit trusts. This is riskier, because values can go up and down. Historically, over periods of ten years or so, you would have consistently beaten inflation if you had invested in good quality UK unit trusts, but if you had had to sell them at the wrong moment to meet a particular need, you could have lost a considerable amount of money. Moreover, there is no guarantee that what has happened in the past will be repeated in the future. However, many people do believe that if investments are made in good class companies, they will continue to make profits above the average and invest in assets that also go up in value. It is these types of investments that form a very large proportion of the portfolios of insurance companies and pension funds. You must bear in mind that in any investment of this type there may be a substantial fall in the short term; it should therefore be considered medium to long term. Anyone unwilling or unable to accept the risk should avoid it altogether.

for how long must you invest

Investments vary considerably in when you can get your money back. Building society share accounts, for example, give instant access; there are many other kinds of accounts with varying periods of notice required. National Savings certificates, while encashable on demand, are only worth having if they can be held for five-yearly periods. Friendly society bonds really need to be held for ten years, guaranteed income bonds with life insurance companies would not be encashable for between two and ten years, depending on the contract.

Think carefully before investing in any scheme which requires you to tie up your money. Some high-interest building society accounts will allow an early withdrawal only with a severe penalty.

Assets-backed investments, such as shares and unit trusts, can be sold at any time, but of course the value might be low just when the money is needed.

tax on investments

The two types of tax which affect investments are income tax and capital gains tax. Careful planning can also be used to alleviate inheritance tax.

income tax

When choosing an investment, you have to take into account how the income is taxed. A few types of investment income are tax-free, most kinds are taxable. Taxable investment income is added to your earned income and taxed in the normal way.

The tax on taxable investment income is gathered by the Inland Revenue in one of three ways.

1   With a few types of investment, the income is paid out to you gross with no tax deducted; anybody who has to pay tax on this income then pays it either in their bill or through PAYE.

2   Other types of investment pay out an income after basic rate tax has been deducted. If you are a non-taxpayer even after this income is taken into account, or should pay less tax than has been deducted, you can claim tax back. If you are a higher rate taxpayer, you will have to pay extra tax.

3   The majority of savings accounts operated by banks, building societies and finance companies deduct the equivalent of basic rate tax, at a special composite rate (fixed at 23.25% for the 1988/89 tax year), before paying out an income. This rate is usually below the basic rate to take account of those non-taxpayers who nevertheless invest in such accounts. Such people cannot reclaim this tax, and higher rate taxpayers have to pay more. To work out the before-tax amount of this type of income (the gross amount), you have to 'gross up' the interest you get, by dividing it by 0.75. For example, if the interest payments you get in a tax year amount to £375, the grossed up amount of interest is £500.

For this reason, non-taxpayers should invest in accounts where the interest is paid gross. They should bear in mind that even if they can reclaim tax, from dividends for instance, they may have to wait for some time until their rebate arrives.

Higher rate taxpayers should consider putting their money into tax-free investments, or investments which are taxed as capital gains rather than income, provided that they are not making full use of their capital gains tax allowance.

age allowance

If you are retired, you pay tax like anyone else but if you are over 64 at the start of the tax year (or are a married man whose wife is), you can claim the age allowance (in the 1988/89 tax year £3,180 or £5,035 if married) instead of the normal personal allowance, which is less. For those aged 79 or more at the start of the the tax year, the age allowance rises to £3,310 and £5,205 respectively.

However, once what is called your 'total income' reaches a certain amount (£10,600 in the 1988/89 tax year) your age allowance is reduced rather sharply. For every £3 by which your 'total income' exceeds the (£10,600) limit, you lose £2 of your age allowance, until the allowance is reduced to the level of the ordinary personal allowance. It can never be reduced to less than this amount. (At present this is £2,605 for a single person, £4,085 for a married man.)

To work out your 'total income', add up your gross income for the tax year:

○ both husband's and wife's incomes
○ the grossed up amount of any interest from which the equivalent of any basic rate tax has been deducted before you get it, for example building society or bank interest
○ any taxable gain on a life insurance policy (with some exceptions – see single premium investment bonds)

then deduct:

○ interest you pay which qualifies for tax relief (for example, interest on the mortgage to buy your home, or home improvement loans taken out before the 1988 budget)
○ contributions you pay to a personal pension plan
○ half the amount of any class 4 National Insurance contributions you pay
○ the gross amount of any covenant payments and enforceable maintenance payments you make and have been making since before the 1988 Budget.

try to save your age allowance
If your income is so high that each extra £ of taxable income loses you some age allowance, extra care may be necessary when choosing your investments. Consider putting some of

your money into tax-free investments. After the saving of tax and age allowance is taken into account, the return may be better than that for an investment with a higher rate of return at face value.

claiming income tax back

If you have investment income from which basic rate tax is deducted before you get it and you are a non-taxpayer or your tax bill should be less than the amount of tax deducted, you should claim a rebate. With dividends from shares and most unit trust distributions, the payments will be accompanied by a tax voucher showing that you get a tax credit. If your tax bill comes to less than the total of tax deducted plus tax credits received, you will have paid too much tax and should also claim a tax rebate.

If the Inland Revenue consider that you will be able to claim a rebate, you may receive a special tax claim form (R40) instead of the normal kind of tax return. You should fill it in and send it back with the tax vouchers you get with the income. You do not need to wait until the end of the tax year to do this; claim as soon as you have received all your relevant investment income for the tax year.

The taxman will work out how much overpaid tax you are owed, if any, and send you a rebate. Arrangements can be made for repayment of tax by instalments during the year; ask your tax office for details .

If you have to claim tax back regularly, but are not sent form R40 automatically, ask your tax office for it. Some tax offices now send a form R40 at the same time as the tax rebate so you can send it off to them next year as soon as you are ready.

capital gains tax

You make a capital gain whenever you part with something for more than you paid for it. However, most people are unlikely to have to worry about capital gains tax on their investments, because

○ some investments are tax-free altogether
○ only gains made since 31 March 1982 will be taxable
○ an indexation allowance prevents you being taxed on any gain made purely as a result of inflation
○ capital losses you make are deducted from capital gains in any tax year and net losses may also be carried forward from earlier years to be deducted from gains made; this reduces the amount on which you pay tax
○ a certain amount of capital gain you make is free of tax (in the 1988/89 tax year this is the first £5,000). From 1990, wives and husbands will have a separate allowance each.

If you do have to pay capital gains tax, it is payable at the same rate as your top income tax rate; either 25% or 40%.

Capital gains made on the following types of investment are tax-free:

○ the sale of your only or main home (if you have more than one home, you can choose which one you want to count as your main home; it does not have to be the one you live in most of the time)
○ investments passed from husband to wife, or vice versa; it could be worth making changes in this respect now, to take advantage of the separate allowances from 1990
○ National Savings of any kind
○ premium bond prizes
○ proceeds from life insurance policies, unless you bought the policy from a previous holder
○ British government stocks
○ the sale of personal belongings, antiques, jewellery, and other movable objects, provided the value of any one object when you sell it is not more than £3,000.

There are other reliefs available, such as when making gifts where tax can be deferred until their subsequent disposal (for example, if you give shares to your son – or anyone else – tax can be deferred until he sells them).

your own business

Tax reliefs are allowed for people selling their own businesses on retirement. Whenever the situation appears complicated or there is doubt, professional advice should be sought.

People aged 60 or more, or who have to retire early through ill health, may obtain retirement relief for capital gains tax on the disposal of a business. Disposal of part can also be eligible for relief. The relief is given on gain relating to 'chargeable business assets'. In addition, it applies to people who held shares in a family trading company provided the person has been a full-time working director for a year. Otherwise the business must have been owned for at least a year. Relief may be granted if a full-time working director disposes of an asset used rent-free by his or her family company for the purposes of its trade, provided that the disposal is associated with a disposal of shares in the company.

which type of investment?

Here is a brief outline of the main types (in alphabetical order, not in order of priority).

annuities

You can buy an annuity with a lump sum from a life insurance company. It gives you a guaranteed income either for a set number of years (perhaps 5 years) or – a life annuity – will continue until you die. It can be for 'joint lives' for a married couple, to continue until the second one dies. Annuities for couples are known as joint life and survivor annuities, and pay out less than those for a single person.

The older you are when buying an annuity, the better the value because the income is based on life expectancy. Women usually get less than men of the same age because they are thought to tend to live longer. For example, in return for £10,000 invested in January 1989, a 65 year old man who paid tax at the basic rate could have got an after-tax income of about £1,236 a year for life, a 65 year old woman £1,088. A 75 year old man would have got £1,662, while a 75 year old woman would have got £1,452 a year.

Most companies give a choice of how often the payments are made – annually, quarterly or monthly – and you can some-times choose whether they are paid in advance or arrears. If they are paid more frequently than once a year, each payment is lower, pro rata, so this will mean a slightly lower income in total.

There are a number of different types of annuity. Apart from the level kind, which does not increase in value, there is also an increasing annuity. This generally has a built-in increase of either 5% or 8½% a year; in the case of the former, it will take some 6 or 7 years before it pays the same income as a level one, but will then continue increasing your income steadily. The 8½% increase type starts at a much lower level.

Deferred annuities are also available. With these, the income only starts some time after you have made the payment – 5 years, say. By buying in advance, you get a higher income when the payments actually start. This type of annuity does involve some risk because the income available from an annuity varies from time to time in line with interest rates in general. You may therefore find that you bought your annuity at a bad time.

With the basic type of annuity, if you were to die shortly after taking it out, all your capital would be lost. It is possible to guard against this by taking out what is known as a capital protected annuity. In this case, as a minimum, the balance of the investment not paid out will be repaid to your estate in the event of your death. With another type, the payments continue after you die, also to your estate, to the total minimum value of your original investment. Because of the guarantee involved, with these annuities the income will be lower.

You can also buy with-profits and unit-linked annuities. With these, the purchase money is invested in with-profits or unit-linked investment funds.

This means that you get a slightly lower income to start with, but if the funds in which the money is invested do well, you may get an increased income later from investment bonuses, and increases in the value of the units, which will help protect your income against inflation.

Current rates of annuities are shown in trade magazines such as *Planned Savings, Money Management*, and *Savings Market* (which you will find in your local reference library). Rates change extremely rapidly, however, particularly in volatile market conditions, so it is advisable to check with one or two brokers for up-to-date figures and if you decide to invest, to make the decisions quickly once you have the quotation.

annuities: tax
Provided that you buy the annuity voluntarily, with your own money and not as part of your pension scheme, only part of the income is taxable and counts towards your 'total income' for tax purposes.

Part of the income from an annuity is treated as a return of capital and is therefore tax-free. The other part is treated as interest on your lump sum, and this is taxed as investment income. Basic rate tax is usually deducted before you get the payments. Non-taxpayers can ask to have the income paid without this deduction. But beware! some inspectors of taxes are reluctant to grant this concession and if you come across this problem, ask the insurance company to provide an appropriate letter, which can usually circumvent this diffi- culty. Higher rate taxpayers will have to pay some extra tax.

With an annuity which you buy as part of a personal pension plan, the whole payment is treated as earned income.

annuities: pros and cons
The payments are guaranteed. Although annuity rates vary, you continue to receive the rate that applied when you bought your annuity, so will do comparatively well or badly depending on how interest rates change after you buy the annuity. You will do best if interest rates are high when you take one out and they then fall. Unless you choose an increasing annuity, or one linked to a with-profits or unit-linked fund, the purchasing power may be eaten away by inflation. However, an annuity is basically a gamble. With most types, if you die, however soon after buying one, your family gets nothing back (and paying for a protected or guaranteed annuity means a lower income). You may be willing to put up with these risks for the sake of a guaranteed income. But the income available at younger ages means it is not worth buying an annuity below the age of 70, at least.

bank investments

The high street banks offer a large and varied range of investments, many of which are very similar to those offered by building societies and finance companies. With many accounts nowadays, the more you have invested, the higher the interest rate. Many banks offer facilities such as cash machine cards on some of their savings accounts.

bank deposit accounts have the advantage that the minimum you can invest is generally very low, it may be as little as £1. The interest rate is usually low too, and the equivalent of basic rate tax is deducted before you get it. Even non-taxpayers cannot reclaim this tax. In theory, with most deposit accounts you have to give 7 days' notice if you want to get your money out. In practice, the bank will pay out on the spot, but some banks deduct 7 days' interest unless you use your cash machine card for the withdrawal. Interest is worked out on a daily basis and is usually added to your account twice or 4 times a year.

higher rate deposit accounts: in return for a higher minimum investment of, say, £1,000 (which you must not fall below) you get a higher interest rate than for an ordinary deposit account, and can get your money out at once.

high interest cheque accounts offer some banking facilities, such as a cheque book, and an interest rate higher than for an ordinary account. However, a charge may be made for issuing more than a few cheques per half year, and often there is a minimum value that can be drawn. You can get your money back on demand, but there is usually a high minimum investment of around £1,000 upwards. The interest rate is sometimes on a sliding scale depending on how much is in the account.

fixed notice or penalty accounts: when you invest your money, you agree to give a fixed period of notice, say 28 days, before you cash it in. In return, you get a higher interest rate than for an ordinary deposit account. You may be able to get your money back at once, by losing interest. The minimum investment varies, but may be around £1,000.

fixed term accounts are offered by all banks; for some, interest is paid gross for amounts over £50,000. You invest for a set period of time – say 1, 2, 3, or 6 months or a year – and cannot withdraw the money earlier. They differ from other bank investments in that the rate of interest is fixed at the time you open the account, and remains the same for the duration. This gives you the certainty of a fixed income, but whether or not it proves to be the best return will depend on how rates change after you invest. The minimum investment is unlikely to be less than about £5,000 with a very high maximum. They can be ideal for people who have just sold a house and need a safe haven for their money for a short period before buying another, for example.

regular savings accounts are offered by a few banks. You agree to save a set amount – for example £10 a month. Withdrawal conditions and interest vary from bank to bank.

bank investments: tax
Most bank interest is taxed in the same way as building society interest – that is, by the deduction of the composite rate tax. This tax cannot be reclaimed; higher rate taxpayers will have to pay extra tax.

bank investment: pros and cons
The income from bank investments is generally variable and, because it comes in the form of interest rather than capital gain, there is no protection against inflation. The great variety of bank accounts now means that you may be able to find rates of interest as good as those offered by building societies – in fact, in the autumn of 1988, a number of them were considerably better. (But bank ordinary deposit accounts are rarely competitive). Roughly speaking, the more money you have to invest, the higher the interest rate – although you can also get higher interest rates if you are prepared to tie your money up for some time. Some bank savings accounts also offer the convenience of banking facilities, such as cheque books and cash machine cards. Non-taxpayers should remember that they cannot reclaim the tax deducted from the interest.

British government stocks

The government issues these (also known as gilt-edged securities, commonly shortened to 'gilts') as a way for them to borrow money. There have been far fewer of these issues in the last 2 years than formerly, because the government has had less need to borrow.

The prices of gilts are quoted as the price for each £100 of nominal stock. When gilts are first issued, the price is usually quite close to £100 per £100, which is known as par. However, very often they are issued at a slight discount, say £97.50 per £100 in order to give initial investors an incentive. The government promises to redeem them at face value at a set date, which can be as distant as 2024 or as close as 1990. In the meantime, the holder gets a set amount of interest, usually twice a year. There are a few undated gilts but these are invariably historical and in one case, the well known $3\frac{1}{2}$% War Loan started off with a date, but the government then asked people to reinvest undated (actually 1947 or after – but after has never come). In the meantime, the holder gets a set amount of interest, usually twice a year.

You can buy gilts when first issued; when there is a new issue of government stock, watch out for advertisements in the newspapers. You can buy direct by filling in a coupon from newspapers such as the *Financial Times*, the *Guardian*, the *Independent*, the *Times* and the *Daily Telegraph*, and do not have to pay brokerage. You could then hold them until maturity, which makes them a safe way of getting a set income from a lump sum. Alternatively, you can buy them after they have first been issued or sell them before they mature, on the stock exchange. You can buy and sell through a stockbroker, bank or other investment adviser (in which case you will have to pay commission but at a lower rate than that on shares). If you do this, the price can vary – it can be above the nominal value or below. Roughly speaking, the price of gilts falls if interest rates in general rise, and vice versa. So you can also use them as a speculative way of investing, and make a capital gain (or loss) when you sell them, depending on the price at which you buy and sell. You can, for certain gilts only, buy through the National Savings Stock Register, at a very low commission. However in this case it is not possible to buy at a certain price or make a limit order. A limit order is an order to a stockbroker to buy or sell stocks or shares at a certain price or better.

You can get more details about this and an application form at your local post office. You may see a certain number of gilts issued at an interest rate well below the going rate. These are usually intended for higher rate taxpayers who will not mind foregoing interest on the chance of making a tax-free capital gain.

You can also get index-linked gilts. If you hold the stock from when it was issued until it is redeemed, it is guaranteed to keep pace with inflation. At redemption, it is worth the face value of the stock increased in line with inflation over the lifetime of the stock. These invariably have a low interest rate (or coupon as the professionals call it) but this also increases slightly during the lifetime of the stock.

So, the return from British government stocks can come as

○ regular income (normally fixed), some stocks, known as 'high coupon' stocks pay out a high income; 'low coupon' stocks pay you a low income so they are more attractive to higher rate taxpayers or people who do not want a high income but are more interested in making a capital gain
○ capital gain (or loss) if you buy the stock after it is issued or sell it before it is redeemed. With index-linked stocks kept to redemption, there is guaranteed protection against inflation.

British government stocks: tax
Interest is payable after deduction of basic rate tax. However, if the stock is purchased through the National Savings Stock Register, interest will be paid gross. This is ideal for non-tax-payers. The interest will still have to be declared to the Inland Revenue if you are liable to pay tax. Higher rate tax payers will have to pay more whether or not the interest is paid gross. Any capital gain made on selling is free of tax.

British government stocks: pros and cons
British government stocks are a versatile investment which can
be used either to provide a safe and regular income for a fixed
period, or as a more risky way of making a capital gain (or loss).
They are not suitable if you might need your money in a hurry.
If interest rates go down generally, to below the interest rate of
your gilts, you could do very well both because you continue
to get a comparatively high income, and because the price of
the stock would be high if you sold. The reverse could apply if
interest rates go up. You can also use index-linked stocks to
guard against inflation.

building society investments

There is a great variety of building society accounts, so it is
worth being prepared to shop around to find the best interest
rate. On most accounts, interest is credited to the account
twice yearly; with some it is credited monthly, which then
increases the income considerably. But with some, the interest
is added only once a year. This can affect the true rate of return
from the account, so that an account crediting the income only
once a year would offer a lower return than one with the same
nominal interest rate which credits the interest twice yearly.
Smaller building societies will often have better rates of
interest.

With most building society accounts, the interest will go up
or down with interest rates in general. Sometimes – but rarely
– you can find building society accounts where the interest rate
is fixed at the time you take it out. Such accounts are normally
only available for a short period.

Although the names given to accounts vary from society to
society, they fall into some basic types:

ordinary share accounts have a low minimum investment –
usually £1 – so can be a good place for saving odds and ends of
money. You can get your money back at once, although the

amount you can draw in cash without notice may be limited (to £250 in cash, say, or £5000 by cheque). If a building society fails, the investor in a share account gets back 90% of the first £20,000 invested.

deposit account is similar to an ordinary share account but you are technically a lender of money to the building society instead of a member. You are therefore guaranteed that all your money will be safe even if the society were to fail. However, the interest rate is usually about $\frac{1}{2}$% less than a share account.

fixed notices or penalty shares: when you invest your money, you agree to give a fixed period of notice, say 28 days, before you cash it in. In return, you get a higher interest rate than for an ordinary deposit or share account. You may be able to get your money back at once, by losing interest. The minimum investment varies, but may be from around £250 upwards.

high interest, no notice shares work exactly as the name suggests, but there is usually a higher minimum investment than for ordinary shares. The more you can invest, the higher the interest rate. With some, there is an even higher interest if you do not withdraw the money for a whole year.

subscription share accounts are suitable for saving a regular sum of money – say £10 a month. The accounts vary widely from society to society; there are usually restrictions on when you can withdraw the money.

monthly income accounts: are offered by some building societies, often as variations on their normal accounts. You may have to make a bigger initial investment to qualify.

building society investments: tax
There is no basic rate tax to pay on the interest you get from a building society investment because the composite rate tax is deducted at source. If you are a non-taxpayer, you cannot claim back the deducted tax. If you are a higher rate taxpayer, you will have to pay extra tax on the grossed-up income.

building society investments: pros and cons

The income from building society accounts is not fixed but depends on the economic climate. It comes in the form of interest, not capital gain, so there is no protection against inflation. However, you cannot make a capital loss. The investments are safe because there is an Investor Protection Fund: if your society fails, you will get back 90% of the first £20,000 you invested.

You can get a good interest rate by shopping around – particularly if you have around £1000 or more to invest. You are not tied to your building society: if another one offers a better deal, you can withdraw your investments (unless they are on fixed notice), and place them where the interest rates are higher.

Non-taxpayers should remember that they cannot reclaim the tax deducted from the interest.

business expansion scheme

The BES scheme was set up by the government to encourage investment in new or small companies which find it difficult to raise money. Under the scheme, you buy either shares in one such company or make an investment in a scheme similar to a unit trust which is run by a finance house. In this case, the finance house invests in a number of such companies. Such schemes are often offered towards the end of a tax year.

Tax relief is given on your investment at your top rate of tax (which could be at 40%) when the company issues the appropriate certificate.

The investment has to be held for 5 years before it can be realised and there is no guarantee that the shares will then be saleable or quoted on the stock exchange.

The investment is a very high risk one because many such companies have gone bust; others, however, have been extremely successful and gone up in value many times.

business expansion scheme: tax

There is tax relief on the initial investment at the highest rate of tax. If any dividends are payable they will be taxed in the normal way, but as the investments are in the early days of companies, it is unlikely that there will be income for some years.

business expansion scheme: pros and cons

This is a very high risk investment, which may however suit people who like a speculation. The tax relief element is a sweetener but you must be prepared to lose all your money.

finance company (or finance house) investments

There is a considerable variation between the savings accounts offered by finance companies; some are very similar to those offered by the high street banks. Make sure you invest your money only with a company that is a 'licensed deposit taker', that is, licensed by the Bank of England and having to meet certain requirements. There is a deposit protection fund, which will pay out 90% of the first £20,000 you have invested if a licensed deposit taker were to fail. A deposit taker which is not licensed would have to be based outside the UK (which could mean the Isle of Man or the Channel Islands), but it is not worth leaving the protection of UK laws for the extra money you may get by investing in offshore funds.

Finance houses accounts include

deposit accounts (or notice accounts): usually you have to tie up your money for a minimum period and give notice before withdrawing your money. The notice period can range from one month to a year. The minimum investment is likely to be from around £500 upwards.

money market accounts (or money funds): in return for a high maximum investment (anything from £1000 to £10,000), you get a high interest rate. The rate varies from time to time. You can get your money back at once, or at a few days' notice.

finance company investments: tax
Interest from finance company deposits is taxed in the same way as building society and bank interest. Composite rate tax is deducted from the interest before it is paid. Even people who should not pay tax will not be able to reclaim this tax; higher rate taxpayers will have to pay higher rate tax on the grossed up amount of the income.

finance company investments: pros and cons
Many different accounts are available. There is no protection against inflation (because there is no chance of a capital gain). These investments are not suitable for non-taxpayers, unless the after-tax rate of return is higher than they could get elsewhere.

friendly society bonds

These are 10-year savings schemes run by friendly societies. Some of them are linked to building societies, others invest in unit trust type schemes.

Saving through a friendly society has tax advantages which mean that you could enjoy a higher return than with a similar unit-linked insurance contract. However, you must save for the full 10 years and there are penalties for early withdrawal. The plan may be left to accumulate further after the 10 years are up.

The amount that may be saved is strictly limited by the government to £9 per month. (Husbands and wives may both invest £9 a month each.) It is possible to make a lump sum investment of about £820. In this case the sum purchases an annuity which funds the annual premiums. Investments made on an annual basis are usually £100. Apart from the convenience and a small saving overall, most people will do better to invest monthly or annually. The proceeds are free of all tax and no tax is levied on the funds. They are of similar risk to unit trusts or unit linked life insurance.

friendly society bonds: tax
No tax is payable by the investor on maturity and capital gains tax is not levied. In addition, the friendly society does not have to pay tax.

friendly society bonds: pros and cons
They are worth considering as a savings scheme as part of an overall plan. The premiums are modest. The investments could go down as well as up. They must be considered as a 10-year investment, so if there is any doubt as to whether premiums can be maintained, do not invest in one. If it has to be cashed in early, the society is allowed to refund only the premiums, because of the tax concessions. An alternative could be to have the policy made 'paid up' and allow it to continue without further premiums.

guaranteed futures accounts

These are a fairly new invention and usually work on the principle that a proportion of your money is invested in a zero coupon stock, often issued in the USA. With this, the interest is not paid out but is 'rolled up', ensuring that there will be guaranteed growth from this bond sufficient completely to repay all of your invested capital at the end of the term, which is usually 5 years. The rest of the money is invested by dealers in 'futures' trading. (That is, an agreement to buy, or sell, raw materials such as metals or coffee/cocoa/rubber at a specified date in the future at a price fixed now.) No income is payable but there is the chance of a capital gain. In any event, there is a guarantee that all your capital will be repaid, but if no gain is made, you will not keep up with inflation.

guaranteed futures accounts: tax
No income tax is payable on the investment (because there is no income) but capital gains tax will be levied if a gain is made.

guaranteed futures accounts: pros and cons
It is really only a suitable investment for small amounts of capital where the income is not important. Lack of income makes it unsuitable for many retired people but the capital gain could be quite substantial. Care needs to be taken to ensure that the company issuing such an investment is sound – check with one or two advisers. There is a high risk/reward ratio.

income bonds

This sort of investment is offered by life insurance companies. You invest a lump sum (usually a minimum of around £1000 upwards) for a set period (between 1 and 10 years). During that time you get a guaranteed income, a percentage of the investment. At the end of the period, but usually not before, you get your original investment back. The rate of interest can initially appear very attractive, but bear in mind that this will be fixed for the period of the bond. The bonds are usually offered by insurance companies which need extra liquidity for some particular purpose, hence the rate being rather more than the usual market one.

There is also another kind of income bond where part of the money is invested in an investment bond. In this case, while you may make a gain when the investment matures, it is possible that the growth on the bond will be insufficient to repay all your capital. This type of investment is one for which advice should be sought before going ahead.

income bonds: tax
The tax treatment depends on how the bond works. As the technical specification of bonds varies, it is best to take advice from the insurance company. Check carefully with the company, before investing, that the proceeds from the bond (that is, the encashment of the bond at the end of the term) will not affect your age allowance.

income bonds: pros and cons
Income bonds offer no protection from inflation – and can affect your age allowance. They do however give the security of a fixed income for an agreed period.

investment trusts

Investment trusts are public limited companies quoted on the stock exchange. They differ from other companies in that instead of owning buildings or machinery, or manufacturing goods or providing services, they exist purely to buy, hold and sell shares in other companies. Buying shares in an investment trust company is a way of spreading your money over a number of company shares but you should carefully compare the difference between investment trusts and unit trusts in this respect.

You get a return in the form of dividends from the investment trust company, usually paid out twice a year. In addition, there is the chance, when you sell, that you will get more for the shares than the amount you paid (and vice versa). So you could make a capital gain (or loss).

You buy shares in an investment trust company in the same way as shares in any other company – through a stockbroker, bank, or other investment adviser. You have to pay commission on the purchase together with stamp duty and one or two other small charges. There is, in theory, no minimum investment, although in practice the level of commissions means that it is probably not worth buying less than £1000-worth or so of shares.

Unlike unit trusts, investment trusts can only issue more shares by a special meeting of its members (i.e. shareholders). They are, therefore, so-called 'closed ended' funds. The shares tend to be bought/sold at a price not linked to the underlying value of the shares but at a discount according to the trust's popularity with investors.

With one or two companies, you can invest directly through monthly savings schemes. This can be an effective method of building up a nest egg.

investment trusts: tax
Investment trusts are taxed in the same way as other companies. The company deducts basic rate income tax from the dividends before paying them to the shareholders. Non-taxpayers can reclaim this tax; higher rate taxpayers will have to pay more income tax. If you make a capital gain, you may also have to pay capital gains tax on the profits.

investment trusts: pros and cons
Investment trusts offer the possibility of a capital gain, to protect your income against inflation – but there is also the risk of a capital loss. Do not consider them unless you can afford to lose part of your money, and certainly do not put all your money into investment trusts. If you are prepared to take some risk, they are a sensible alternative to investing in other types of shares, because it is possible to spread a comparatively small amount of money over a larger number of companies in this way.

life insurance savings schemes, unit-linked

These are a way of making regular payments (a 'plan') into a life insurance fund; this buys you shares (units) in the fund.

The value of your units goes up or down in line with the investment performance of the fund. Your plan usually lasts for a set number of years (often 10) after which you have the option of cashing in your units or holding on to them. Some of your payments also go to pay for life insurance; if you die while the plan is running, your estate will get a lump sum – how much depends on your age and the type of scheme – with some also on your state of health.

You can surrender, that is cash in, the plan at any time, but the amount you get back may be very low because the company recoups most of its costs early on. The insurance company makes charges, some of which can be heavily weighted in the first 2 or 3 years. Also, the value of the units can go down as well as up so, for this reason too, you may get back less than you invested.

Because of this, you should only consider one of these schemes if you are prepared to carry on investing for 10 years or so.

The minimum you can invest can be anything from £5 a month upwards.

life insurance savings schemes, unit-linked: tax

The lump sum you get from the plan on maturity or death is free of basic rate tax (the insurance company is deemed to have already paid on its investments) and free of capital gains tax (unless – which is rare – you bought the policy from a previous holder). Higher rate taxpayers may have to pay higher rate income tax if the policy is cashed in during its first 10 years or in the first three-quarters of the time it was planned to last for, if shorter.

If you took out a policy before 14 March 1984 you may be getting a $12\frac{1}{2}\%$ subsidy on the premiums, known as life assurance premium relief. You may lose this subsidy if you alter the policy so as to increase the benefits.

life insurance saving schemes, unit-linked: pros and cons
If you are prepared to treat them as a long-term investment, unit linked life insurance schemes can be a way of making a capital gain (or a capital loss). Charges can be heavy in the first few years of the scheme. If you are not prepared to tie your money up for long enough, consider unit trusts or investment trusts instead. If you want to take less of a risk, the answer may be to take out a with-profits scheme instead. Because prices of the units can go up and down, be careful when you cash in. It may be possible to freeze the plan on maturity without paying further premiums and allow it to grow or encash it when conditions are more favourable. If all you want is life insurance, other policies are more suitable.

life insurance savings schemes, with-profits

You pay regular amounts to a life insurance company which invests your money in a fund. In return, the company guarantees to pay a set amount at the end of the scheme, or if you die while it is running. You also get regular bonuses added to this guaranteed amount. The amount of the bonus depends on how the investments in the fund are doing. The company may also pay a terminal bonus when the policy matures. In recent years, these terminal bonuses have been very high, but since the crash of 1987 there is a possibility that these will be lower. There is no guarantee that they will continue at the previous figures or even that there will still be any. Some companies are now issuing with-profits policies which are unitised and operate rather like unit-linked ones, except that bonuses cannot be taken away. The latest trend is towards adding bonuses on a much more frequent basis, but without a terminal bonus at all, and in the long run this may benefit the investor.

The minimum you can invest is usually from £10 a month upwards, and the minimum length of time for which such policies run is usually 10 years. You may be able to cash it in earlier, but because a company recoups most of its costs in the early years, the amount you get may be very small, or even less than the amount paid in, particularly in the first 5 years of the policy.

Some schemes are particularly geared to house purchase and are known as low cost schemes in which more of the money is used for life insurance than for investment. They can, of course, also be used for other purposes.

life insurance savings schemes, with-profits: tax

The lump sum you get from the plan is free of basic rate tax. If you are a higher rate taxpayer you may have to pay higher rate tax if you cash in the policy in its first ten years, or in the first three-quarters of the time it is planned to last for, if shorter. The proceeds are free of capital gains tax unless you bought the policy from a previous holder.

If you took out a policy before 14 March 1984 you may be getting life assurance premium relief at 12½% deduction. You may lose this subsidy if you alter the policy so as to increase the benefits.

life insurance saving schemes, with-profits: pros and cons

With-profits endowment policies give a steady return, with the chance of beating inflation. Your family also gets a lump sum if you die while the policy is running (though if all you want is life insurance, this is not the best kind of policy). Once added to the policy, bonuses cannot be taken away. So this sort of life insurance saving scheme is slightly less risky than a unit-linked life insurance plan. On the other hand, the life insurance company may need to keep back for a rainy day some of the investment profits from a with-profits fund, while with a unit-linked policy more of the profits are likely to be passed on. A with-profits saving scheme should be treated as a long-term investment.

local authority investments

There are three main sorts of investments:

loans to local authorities last for a fixed term, usually between 1 and 7 years. The local authority pays interest on the loan – the amount is fixed when you take out the loan. Once you have invested the money, you cannot usually get it back until the end of the agreed period. The minimum investment is generally, £1000.

local authority stock is rather like British government stock. When it is first issued it can be bought direct from the local authority. After that, it can be bought or sold on the stock exchange, and the price goes up or down. You could make a capital gain (or a capital loss). Alternatively you could hang on to the stock until it matures, when you will get the face value of the stock. There is no minimum investment in theory, but because of the cost of buying and selling, the minimum sensible investment is around £1000.

yearling bonds work in a similar way to local authority stock, but usually last for a short time, most commonly 1 year. They may be called local authority negotiable bonds and are usually sold in multiples of £1000.

local authority investments: tax
Interest on loans to local authorities is taxed in the same way as bank and building society interest. The composite of basic rate tax is deducted before you get the interest, and cannot be reclaimed, even by non-taxpayers. Higher rate taxpayers have to pay extra tax.

The income from local authority stocks and yearling bonds has had basic rate tax deducted before you get it, and higher rate taxpayers have to pay extra tax on it. But non-taxpayers can reclaim tax if their tax bill, including the income, is less than the tax deducted.

There may be capital gains tax to pay on local authority stocks or yearling bonds.

local authority investments: pros and cons

Loans to local authorities have the advantage of offering a set income for a fixed period. They provide no protection against inflation, and you cannot get your money back before the fixed period. Non-taxpayers should remember that they cannot reclaim tax from the interest.

Local authority stocks and yearling bonds on the other hand, do offer the chance of a capital gain – provided that you are happy to take the risk of making a capital loss instead: the price may be low when you want to cash them in.

Local authority investments used to be more widely available than they are now.

national savings investments

You can either buy, or get information about, all National Savings investments at most post offices and there are no buying or selling charges. You can also get up to date information by telephoning 01-605 9461.

National Savings investments include:

National Savings ordinary account which gives a low rate of interest – guaranteed to be $2\frac{1}{2}\%$ in 1989. But for each whole calendar month in which you keep £500 or more in the account, the interest rate rises to 5%. Interest is added on 31 December, for the preceding calendar year. An ordinary account may be attractive to a higher rate taxpayer, because the first £70 of interest a year is free of tax. The minimum investment is £5 and you can withdraw up to £100 on demand.

National Savings investment account pays a higher rate of interest than the ordinary one (currently $10\frac{1}{2}\%$ gross), and the minimum investment is £5. But you have to give 1 month's notice to withdraw money. Interest is added on 31 December, for the preceding calendar year.

National Savings certificates (34th issue available in 1989) give you a guaranteed interest rate, which increases the longer you keep the certificates. You cannot withdraw the interest unless you cash in the certificate. You can, however, withdraw part of the value of a certificate (in a multiple of £25) at any time. You get the full advertised return (the equivalent of 7½% a year on the 34th issue) only if you hold the certificates until the end of a set period, normally 5 years. You can cash in certificates before this for a lower return – the repayment value of the certificates increases at the end of the first year, then at the end of each 3 months. If you cash in during the first year, you get back only the original purchase price of the certificate. You can keep your certificates for longer than 5 years, and will then get the 'general extension rate' of interest, which varies from time to time (at present it is 5.01%).

You can buy the certificates in units of £25, and the maximum holding of the 34th issue is 40 units (£1000). You are also allowed to reinvest £10,000 from earlier issues which you have held for at least 5 years. To cash in a certificate, you fill in an application form obtainable from the post office and your repayment is usually put in the post within 8 working days of your application being received.

index-linked National Savings certificates of which the 4th issue, available since February 1987, is still on sale. Like other National Savings certificates, you get a guaranteed rate of return, which increases the longer you keep the certificate (up until the end of the set period, currently 5 years, after which you will get additional 'loyalty bonuses' at a variable rate). The actual interest rate appears to be low at 4.04% a year for the 4th issue but the certificates also guarantee that their value is index-linked at a tax free rate of return which matches the rate of inflation. If you cash them in during the first year, you only get back what you originally paid. If you cash in after that, you get back the value of the certificates increased at the annual inflation rate, plus interest on a sliding scale. The minimum investment is £25 but, unlike other National Savings certificates, the maximum is £5,000 on the 4th issue. They can be bought in multiples of £25 and the £5,000 maximum is in addition to holdings of all other issues of National Savings certificates. Encashment is arranged in the same way as other National Savings certificates.

National Savings income bonds: the minimum investment is £2,000 and the maximum holding £100,000. You get a monthly income (currently at 11.5% before tax, but the rate can change). You can cash in bonds in multiples of £1000, provided that you leave £2,000 invested, but you have to give 3 months' notice. If you cash in during the first year, you get only half the interest rate from the date of purchase to the date of repayment on the amount repaid.

National Savings capital bonds (Series A) have replaced the deposit bonds which were withdrawn from sale on 19 November 1988. The minimum investment is £100, there is no upper limit as long as you buy in multiples of £100. They offer a guaranteed return equivalent to a compound interest of 12% per annum over a 5-year period. The annual rate of interest after 1 year is $5\frac{1}{2}$% rising to $14\frac{1}{2}$% in the fifth year. After 5 years, no further interest is added, so the bond should then be encashed. They can be cashed before the 5 years are up, with 3 months' notice. The rate of interest increases each year to encourage investors to hold them to the end of the 5 year period.

These bonds may have appeal for non-taxpayers. They have a serious drawback for tax payers, as tax is charged each year even though the interest has only been added on and not paid out. In the last year when the yield is high, this could be punitive for a higher rate tax payer. Advice should be sought as to whether they are suitable for your own circumstances. Because there are no special benefits for higher rate taxpayers (as there is with the tax-free savings certificate), there is no restriction on the maximum holding.

Premium bonds (*'ERNIE'*): the minimum purchase is £10 (for ten bonds), they can be bought up to a maximum of £10,000 in multiples of £5. Each £1 gives you one chance of winning a prize in every draw after you have held them for 3 months. (There are weekly and monthly draws with winnings from £50 to £250,000). The chance of a single £1 bond unit winning a prize is 11,000 to 1 in each monthly draw, so if you were to hold the maximum (£10,000) the odds of winning something are just over evens every month.

Although perhaps not a totally serious method of investment, they may be worth considering for the higher rate taxpayer, because all prizes are tax free. However, do not invest in ERNIES unless you do not care whether you get any income from them or not. Encashment is arranged through the post office – for each £1 you get back £1 (and if you have held them for some years, inflation will have eroded their value).

National Savings yearly plan is a regular savings scheme with a guaranteed return. You make monthly payments of between £20 and £200 a month by standing order, for the first year, after which you are issued with a 'yearly plan certificate'. Interest is then added to the amount built up for a further 4 years. To get the maximum rate of return (which is currently equivalent to $7\frac{1}{2}$% a year) you have to keep the money in the plan for the full 5 years. You can go on investing after the 5 years and you will be advised of a new rate of interest at the time. You can cash the certificate in early, but if you do so during the first year, you get no interest. Your repayment is normally put in the post within 14 working days of your application being received.

National savings investments: tax
The return from National Savings certificates, index-linked National Savings certificates, yearly plan, premium bonds, and the first £70 of interest from an ordinary account, is completely tax free. The return from all other National Savings investments is taxable, but it is paid out to you without any tax being deducted.

National Savings investments: pros and cons

The safety of National Savings investments makes them a useful part of a portfolio, and some offer an attractive interest rate. The tax-free investments are particularly attractive to higher rate taxpayers and people who are close to, or starting to, lose the age allowance. Even the taxable investments are worth considering, especially for non-taxpayers, because they are among the few investments that are paid out before tax is deducted. The income bonds have the advantage of giving a monthly income, and index-linked National Savings certificates provide a hedge against inflation. However, there are restrictions and possibly financial losses if you want to cash in some National Savings investments early.

personal equity plans (PEPS)

This form of investment was introduced by the Finance Act 1986 and has been available since 1 January 1987. Plans are issued by 'plan managers' – insurance companies, banks and unit trust companies. The object was stated by the Chancellor "to encourage people who had never done so before, to invest in shares".

PEPS are in some ways similar to a mini unit trust because your money is spread over a number of investments, but unlike similar plans, they are entirely free of tax if held for at least one calendar year. (The year runs from January to December, unlike other arrangements.) Not only are any capital gains made not assessed for tax, but any dividends earned have the tax reclaimed and added to the plan.

They are, however, riskier than straightforward unit trusts or similar collective investments because, generally, the number of investments that are made are limited to only a few companies. One or two companies allow the investor to choose which of their shares to invest in, but the list may be strictly limited. Some PEPs allow investment in a unit or investment trust but this is limited by the government to £540 or one-quarter of your total PEP investment, whichever is greater. The rest has to be in shares. Some plans operated by unit trust groups will invest the limited amount only in one of their own unit trusts.

For the tax year 1988/89, the limit for a PEP is £3,000 per person. Husband and wife can each have a plan. It is possible to increase the amount of the plan through rights issues that may be declared on the underlying shares.

personal equity plans: tax
The plans are entirely free of any taxes at all if held for at least one January to December twelvemonth.

personal equity plans: pros and cons
All the paperwork is taken care of by the plan manager, but you pay a fairly high setting-up fee and dealing charges. PEPs are well worth considering for people who have used up their capital gains tax allowance provided they can accept the long-term nature of this type of investment. If invested over several years, quite large holdings can be built up and the tax-free treatment could prove to be very attractive, balanced against the risks.

shares

To get the best out of shares, it is essential to have a portfolio, that is, a range of investments which effectively means investing in several companies. The two ways in which a return can be made are income in the form of dividends paid by the company and a capital gain when you sell. There is, however, the risk of a loss depending on whether the share price has risen or fallen.

Shares are listed in a number of ways:

a full listing of over 7000 companies the shares of which are dealt with on the London stock exchange, including so-called 'blue chips' (namely the larger, safer companies), and also unknown – possibly unsound – companies

the unlisted securities market was set up in November 1980 for companies that were not able to produce sufficient information for a full listing. In it are much younger companies, with only a 3-year trading record required, which therefore will tend to be riskier

the third tier market started in autumn 1986 and is highly speculative as it is for very young companies and there are only a few companies in the list so far

the over-the-counter market: it is not recommended to buy these types of shares from anybody offering them over-the-counter, if only because there may not be a market to sell them again.

Apart from the over-the-counter (OTC) market, you can buy and sell all shares through stockbrokers, banks or other authorised investment advisers, who charge commission. The minimum commission varies from broker to broker; it is usually £25; above the minimum, it is a percentage. Although there is no minimum investment as such, the cost of dealing means that it is generally not worth investing less than £1000 in one company's shares. In order to reduce your risk of losing money, you should aim to build up a portfolio of shares in 5 to 10 companies as a minimum.

There is no guarantee that even blue chip shares will show a profit, and there is nothing you can do if you lose money by picking the wrong share. The Investors Compensation Scheme does not cover the normal risk of investment – that the value of shares can go down as well as up.

shares: tax
Dividends on shares are paid after basic rate income tax has been deducted. Non-taxpayers or people who should pay less than the tax deducted, can reclaim the tax; higher rate tax-

payers will have to pay more. If you make a capital gain when you sell, there may be capital gains tax to pay.

shares: pros and cons

Shares give you the possibility of making a capital gain to protect your investment against inflation. If chosen correctly, the dividends can provide a regular, if fluctuating, income. With some better companies, the income could continue to increase year after year, but with more speculative investments it is always possible that it might stop altogether and/or that you could lose some of your capital. Invest no more money in shares than you are prepared to lose. In any case, do not put all your money in shares, and do not invest in them if you cannot afford to buy shares in several companies. As for cashing in your investments, do not necessarily plan to do so on a pre-ordained date (such as, for example, the day you retire): this may be a time when share prices are low. So, be prepared to leave your money invested for a long time, because of the fluctuation in price.

Instead of buying shares, consider unit trusts, investment trusts, British government stocks as alternative investments, or let yourself in gently by buying through PEPs.

single premium bonds

Technically, these are non-qualifying life policies, but the life insurance aspect is, to all intents and purposes, irrelevant, because on death they only pay out marginally more than the surrender value (the value of the bond at death). Your money is invested in one or more of several funds the company runs and you can choose the amount put into each fund yourself. Most companies have a basic range, probably UK equity (shares), European, Far East, North American property, fixed-interest, as well as a mixed fund consisting of a composite of the other funds managed by the insurance company. Depending on investment conditions, the company will almost certainly spread the money between property, fixed interest and ordinary shares, which is less risky than a company investing in shares alone.

All companies will allow you to switch from one fund to another, and the first switch in any one year is usually free, with subsequent ones costing a small fee.

Bonds do not normally pay out an income as such, but you can get income by arranging to cash in part of your investment, either from time to time or on a regular basis. As long as you do not cash in more than the equivalent of 5% of your original investment, what you draw out is tax-free at the time because it is deemed by the Inland Revenue to be – and in fact is – a repayment of capital. These 5%'s can be accumulated for 20 years.

You can usually sell your bond at once, or within a month of buying. If the value of the fund in which it is invested has risen, a chargeable event will have occurred from the tax point of view. This is not quite the same as a capital gain from shares or a unit trust. Any gain made is divided by the number of complete years the bond has been in force, to obtain an average, and this figure is added to the investor's income for the year. If it takes him or her into the higher rate tax bracket, this will be applied to the whole of the gain, even if it straddles both rates. Someone who is already in higher rate tax will have to pay increased tax of 15% (the difference between 25% and 40%) on the gain. This method of reducing the amount by spreading the gain over the number of years the policy has run is known as 'top slicing' and must be claimed by the investor ("I claim relief under Section 400 of the Income and Corporation Taxes Act"). Bear in mind that you could, of course, make a loss instead and this cannot be offset against gains made elsewhere.

The minimum investment varies from company to company, but is usually from £1000 upwards; one or two companies accept £500.

single premium bonds: tax
If you wish, you can cash up to 5% of your original investment each year without paying tax at the time, although you may have to pay extra income tax when you finally cash in the bond if you are, or become, a higher rate taxpayer. For this reason it is worth planning when encashments are to be made. Gains when you cash the bond are free of capital gains tax, and of basic rate income tax (but, again, if you are a higher rate taxpayer, extra tax will be payable).

Single premium bonds are particularly useful for people who are already making use of their capital gains tax limit.

single premium bonds: pros and cons
There is no income; you may get a capital gain which you can cash in. Like unit trusts and investment trusts, single premium bonds offer a convenient way to invest in places which would be too risky for a private investor to invest in directly. There is a possibility of making a capital gain to guard against inflation, but there is a possibility of making a loss instead. For this reason these bonds should be regarded as a long-term investment, for money you are unlikely to need at short notice (when prices may be lower). The life insurance company makes an initial charge and annual management charge, similar to unit trusts. The bonds may be written 'in trust' which can be useful for inheritance tax planning.

unit trusts

This is a way of investing in the stocks and shares of UK and foreign companies, and British government stocks; these are sometimes coupled with other fixed-interest investments. You buy units in a trust fund which invests in many companies; if

one company does badly, this affects only part of your investment. The 'performance' of the shares is reflected in the price
of the units, which can go up or down.

Your return comes in the form of:

Income paid in the form of 'distributions', made up from
dividends from the shares the unit trust invests in. You can
usually choose to have the income reinvested in more units
rather than paid out. If you have bought 'accumulation' units,
you do not get income but the amount of the dividends is
reflected in the unit price.

A capital gain (or loss, depending on whether the price of
your units rises or falls). The success of your investments
depends on the state of the market when you buy and sell.

Some unit trusts concentrate on providing a high income,
others on providing high growth; you can choose which type –
income or growth – suits your needs better. Growth trusts will
tend to do very well in a bull market (which is one which is
going up) but will fall more spectacularly in a bear market
(which is one that is going down).

You can choose between general trusts, which invest in a
wide spread of companies, and trusts which specialise in
investing in another country or area of the world, for example
the USA, Europe, the Far East and so on. Roughly speaking, the
more specialist funds are more risky than general funds, but
can produce the highest growth (or loss).

You can buy direct quite simply (no need for a broker)
through coupons in a newspaper advertisement, for example,
or by post. Unit trust companies make an initial charge and an
annual management charge. You do not pay this separately, it
is included in the price of the units; there is a different price for
buying and for selling to take account of these charges. The
minimum investment is generally between £250 and £1000.
Some unit trust companies also run regular savings schemes,
usually with a minimum monthly investment of around £50,
some will accept £20 or so.

Performance tables are regularly published in the specialised financial press. You can also seek the help of an independent financial adviser who generally will make no charge for this service, because of the commission paid by the unit trust group. An adviser should be able to show you performance graphs of unit trusts you are interested in. Because it is advisable to invest for a minimum of 3 years, preferably more, look at tables of a similar length of time; short-term performance can be very misleading.

unit trusts: tax
Income from a unit trust is paid after basic rate income tax has been deducted. Non-taxpayers and people who should pay less tax than has been deducted, can claim tax back; higher rate taxpayers will have to pay more income tax. You may have to pay capital gains tax on any capital gain.

unit trusts: pros and cons
Because of the possibility of making a capital gain, unit trusts can protect your money against inflation. It is also a convenient way of investing abroad if that appeals to you. Since you could lose part of your money, only invest as much money as you can afford to lose, and do not invest in just one unit trust. Be prepared to treat them as long term investments.

decision time

Before investing any money on retirement, amongst the points to be taken into account are:

○ Is there sufficient income from pensions etc to maintain a comfortable lifestyle?

○ Is the existing income protected against inflation in any way?
○ Are there known commitments in the future for which money will be required (and when are they – for example, family weddings, anniversaries)?
○ Have you an emergency fund?

emergency fund

Everybody should have an emergency fund. This is no less true after you retire than beforehand, and is required for the same reasons. Naturally, the size will depend on your own circumstances but, as before retirement, a useful rule of thumb is approximately three months' income.

The obvious choice is a building society share account, bank high-interest account or a reputable finance company. Instant access, or not more than one month's notice, will be necessary.

specific purpose fund

This is a fund for definite future plans such as a replacement car in two years' time, or a visit to relatives in Australia in five years. Safety is paramount and as the time-scale is known, you can choose an investment maturing when required. Suitable funds would include

○ National Savings investments
○ British government stocks maturing at the appropriate moment
○ longer-term savings accounts with banks, building societies or finance companies
○ index-linked investments if a suitable maturity date can be found
○ guaranteed income bond for the appropriate period from an insurance company

funds for boosting your income now

If you have a lump sum available, there are a number of investments for giving you an increased income immediately. These include

○ Annuities, both level and with annual increases of 5% or $8\frac{1}{2}$% and with or without capital protection. You should take professional advice, particularly if you have heirs.
○ Interest-paying accounts with banks, building societies, and finance companies. Interest rates vary considerably and it is worth making comparisons. Remember that you can use a bank other than your normal one for your investment.
○ Local authority investments (although these are less common than they once were).
○ National Savings investment accounts and income bonds.
○ Life insurance company guaranteed income bonds which pay out a fixed income for a number of years; there are not many of these at present and they vary, so you should obtain advice.
○ Offshore gilt funds – but be careful and certainly use only funds operated by well known unit trust groups, because the same compensation as for ordinary funds may not be available if anything goes wrong. Whilst the income is very high, unless you invest when interest rates are high it is likely that the value of your capital will not increase and may well go down.

funds for boosting your income later

In many cases, pensions will not adequately keep up with inflation. Many pension funds, for example, only allow for maximum increases of 4% whatever inflation is doing, although sometimes pension trustees will make occasional ex-gratia increases. Many of the people who retired in the 1960's have found a very real reduction in their incomes. It therefore seems prudent to make provision now to increase your income at a later date. This is even easier if you do not require the money now.

It is well worth considering investing at least part of your money in an index-linked investment. The main alternative is to invest part of the sum for growth, rather than income, to try to get an increase in its value. Perhaps in five or ten years, if you find that you need to boost your income, you could then cash in this investment and reinvest it in an income-producing investment. Suitable investments for this include

○ National Savings capital bonds: these are rather similar to income bonds except that the income is not payable as income, but is rolled up to increase the capital. They are liable to tax.

○ National Savings certificates and index-linked ones: you can cash these in at regular intervals to provide a tax-free income. For new investors, there is a limit of £1000 so the scope is much less than it used to be. However, £10,000 from earlier issues can be re-invested in the current (34th) issue in addition to the £1000 new investment

○ unit trusts: it is important to invest in the right type of units depending on your circumstances

○ single premium investment bonds: the taxation of these is complicated.

○ stocks and shares, including investment trusts: because of the expenses involved in buying and selling these, a portfolio of less than £10,000, or at least £5,000, is probably not worth thinking about. It is difficult to find a stockbroker who is interested in small portfolios. However, the banks are becoming increasingly helpful and most of them have a broker's department. If you wish to buy or sell foreign shares, the banks often can do this through their overseas departments at considerably less expense than going through their own stockbroker. It may be worth asking about this service but it is for the sophisticated investor only.

some protection for the investor if a firm goes bust

A compensation scheme introduced in August 1988 covers you if any authorised investment business you are using collapses. It is run by a company called Investors Compensation Scheme Ltd (3 Royal Exchange Buildings, London EC3V 3NL). You are not covered for investment deals made before 28 August 1988, nor for investment business carried on outside the UK.

The scheme covers authorised dealings only, not any dealings with firms which are not fully authorised. You can check whether a firm is fully authorised by phoning the Securities and Investment Board (SIB) on 01-929 3652.

You can claim only up to £48,000 (made up of 100% of your money on the first £30,000 and 90% on the next £20,000). If you are investing more, you can increase your protection by splitting your investment between companies; this may, however, mean higher charges.

The scheme does not cover the unavoidable risk that the value of shares or other investments can go down as well as up.

building up a portfolio

There is no one investment that can do everything. For most people, a portfolio will be required to include safe investments which guarantee income, as well as riskier ones to obtain the chance of a capital gain, investments which can be cashed in easily and ones which can be tied up for a period in the hope of greater rewards. Some investments have a minimum sum to limit your choice.

If income needs boosting now, obviously a high-yielding safety fund will form part of the investment mix. But if not, investments should be made for growth from which future income will be available. The degree of safety must be assessed and what may be described as the risk/reward ratio.

Here are some points to remember:

○ The greater the chance of gain, the greater the risk. Balance riskier investments with safe ones.
○ If you cannot afford a spread, go for the safer type of investment.
○ Investments offering an income which is out of line with the market invariably bear a greater risk; take advice.
○ Look into your tax position before investing and if you are not sure, take advice.
○ Ascertain how the return is paid before you make the investment and compare the true annual rate of return or compounded annual rate of interest (CAR) with that of others (with many types of investments, such as in building societies, banks and finance companies, CAR is advertised so you can make a comparison). This is similar to APR (annual percentage rate of charge) which is now used for comparing the true rates of interest when borrowing.
○ Do keep some money in an emergency fund.
○ Do not tie up all your money in long term investments; your circumstances may change unexpectedly.
○ Review your investments at least annually. Your circumstances are bound to change and so will the investment climate. Your original decisions are not cast in granite.

index

some other Consumer Publications

Understanding back trouble
gives sensible advice on how to avoid back trouble both at work and play. Prevention is all-important in this area of the body and so we include a range of detailed back-strengthening exercises to minimise the risk of back strain.

For all those people already suffering from problems with their back this book will help them to understand what has happened to them, why, and advice on what to do about it. There is advice on how to cope with a sudden painful attack and treatments, both orthodox, and alternative are discussed.

Understanding stress
provides practical, useful and sensible advice on how to cope with the stresses inherent in the way we live today. It also looks at specific life events such as death, divorce, job loss etc which all rank very high on the stress chart.

It explains how stress can increase the risk of ill health and affect your body. Throughout the book, outside agencies offering more support are listed, and ways of dealing with stress are discussed in detail.

Which? way to buy, sell and move house
is an invaluable guide to what is involved from the day you start looking for a place to live to completion day. It clarifies issues that have to be decided initially, such as location (town v country), type of property (house v flat), size and style. It tells you what to look out for when viewing and goes carefully through the procedure of making an offer, having a valuation and/or survey, conveyancing, exchange of contracts and completion.

Financial aspects are covered with information about mortgages and statutory fees, as well as other incidental costs (which can all add up) involved in moving.

Finally, a timetable for the moving operation itself guides you through what can be a rather traumatic day.

Starting your own business
is the definitive guide for any budding entrepreneur with courage and imagination. It advises on defining precisely what product or skill you have to offer, how to raise the necessary capital and how to cope with the legal requirements to get you on the right road to realising your dream.

Throughout the book there are sources of advice and information to help the small businessman make a success of going it alone.

Getting work done on your house
is a practical guide to successfully having work done on your house from renewing gutters to building an extension. It will help you to minimise the risk of frustration and disappointment sometimes experienced when trying to explain to a professional just what you want done. The whole process, from deciding what job needs to be done to final payment is covered in detail.

It includes hiring a professional or doing it yourself, documents and regulations, specialist treatments and trade associations, and emergency repair work.

How to buy, sell and own shares
is a suitable guide for the absolute beginner or the proficient expert. Its aim is to help you increase your profit and get more enjoyment out of owning your shares.

This book goes through the mechanics of buying and selling, where to go for advice and who to buy through. It explains income tax, capital gains tax and inheritance tax, rights issues, takeovers and mergers.

Buying, owning and selling a flat
gathers together and explains in simple terms all the areas of
law that are of practical concern to both flat owners and people
thinking of buying a flat.

More and more people are buying flats instead of houses
these days and it is important to understand about the different
types of leasehold, maintenance charges, covenants and so on.

This book examines the relationship with the landlord and
neighbours and the pros and cons of buying a flat jointly with
someone else.

Earning money at home
explains everything you need to know about turning your
hobby into a money-making enterprise. Or perhaps you've
always wanted to work at home instead of travelling to the
office everyday. This book shows you what is entailed in the
way of organising your domestic life, insurance (if needed),
keeping accounts, advertising and dealing with customers.

Divorce – legal procedures and financial facts
makes the procedures and regulations involved in the process
of going through a divorce much more accessible to the lay-
person. It covers getting legal advice, conciliation, legal aid
and its drawbacks, the various financial and property orders
the court can make and what can happen to the matrimonial
home.

If there are children involved this book explains how to
calculate needs and resources. It illustrates the effects of alternative financial solutions to various personal situations on
divorce to try to take account of the problems different couples
have to face.

Which? way to save and invest
covers all the important areas of saving and investing from
traditional choices such as National Savings and bank and

building society savings schemes, to unit trusts, unit-linked life insurance and alternative investments like stamps, diamonds and wine.

This book includes investing for children and retirement and will give you the answers to help you find the best home for your money.

CA publications are available from Consumers' Association Castlemead, Gascoyne Way, Hertford SG14 1LH, and from booksellers.